Uni in the USA

The UK Guide to US Universities

by Alice Fishburn

With Anthony Nemecek, Director of The Educational Advisory Service of the US–UK Fulbright Commission
And with a foreword from Stephen Baldock, lately High Master of St Paul's School, London

www.uniintheusa.com

Illustrations by Tim Sanders

LUCAS
PUBLICATIONS

First Edition published 2005
by Lucas Publications Ltd
Bowland House, West Street, Alresford SO24 9AT
ISBN 09532 659 78

A CIP catalogue record for this book is available from the British Library.

Every care has been taken that all information was correct at the time of going to press. The publishers accept no responsibility for any error in detail, inaccuracy or judgement whatsoever.

Designed by smallkandy and Antony Atha
Edited and typeset by PencilSharp
Printed and bound in Great Britain by Butler & Tanner

Thank yous

Without seeming too sentimental, I owe many people a huge debt of gratitude for this book. I stalked British students in America from coast to coast in an attempt to discover their views on American universities. I alienated pretty much every American friend I have over here by demanding their opinions on the SAT. I bored my siblings on the subject by the hour. To all these people – a big thank you. In particular, I would like to thank my British comrades at Harvard – especially Francesco Goedhuis, who has lived through this book and four years of American education with me – neither of them a particularly easy task. I couldn't have done either without him.

I owe much to my two godmothers. Without them neither this book nor my American education would exist. And, to my mother and father, whose excellent job in selecting my godmothers is only one of the many wonderful things they have done for me along the way, thank you.

This book has been aided greatly by the edits of the wonderful Charles Cowling, whose ability to make order out of chaos and sentences out of nonsense was invaluable. My thanks also go to Claire Sauer of PencilSharp for overseeing the copy-editing, proofreading and typesetting, and to Claire Bowles for handling the publicity.

Alice Fishburn, December 2004

Contents

About This Book
and Alice Fishburn

I have a confession to make. I owned a pair of Harvard pyjamas as a child. There are pictures of me looking charming in them and reading Beatrix Potter. My indoctrination in the merits of an American education may well have started at this point, although I am certain I held out for a good many years. But finally, having spent the better part of my teenage years ignoring parental suggestions, I ploughed my way through my Scholastic Aptitude Tests (SATS) as well as my A Levels, submitted my applications and found myself on a plane to Boston. Now, in my final year at Harvard, I am the recipient of an education that has been considerably harder than Peter Rabbit's but just as rewarding. And as the deadly date of graduation creeps ever nearer, I find myself thinking back over the decisions that landed me here.

Harvard Pyjamas
(AS WORN BY THE AUTHOR)
(AS A CHILD...)

Try as I might, I don't think I can blame the pyjamas. Even the skilled psychological tactics of my parents were not the deciding factor. Instead I realized I simply couldn't get what I wanted from England. I had no idea what I wanted to do with my life and the thought that, aged eighteen, I would be limited to one academic subject for the next three years gave me claustrophobia. America, on the other hand, refused to let me confine myself. I had to take a variety of courses – in three years here I have studied physics, Chinese politics and musical theory while majoring in history and literature. I was given the freedom to choose what I wanted to do and the flexibility to go back and correct any initial mistakes (did I really think I wanted a degree in Classics?) The American education offered me the chance both to explore and to specialize – an option of which many undecided students in the UK are simply not aware.

I jumped at the chance to write this book because it gave me the opportunity to dispel several of the myths that persist about college in America. Try as we might, we Brits often cannot refrain from viewing education on that side of the pond with a certain amount of disdain. The thought that I, a quintessentially British girl in both birth and education, would want to throw in my lot with a bunch of Americans came as a nasty surprise to many of my friends and teachers. But what school teachers particularly fail to recognize is that today American universities are some of the most successful and prosperous ones around. Indeed when *The Times Higher Educational Supplement* recently ranked the top ten universities in the world, seven American schools were among that number (a certain amount of school pride requires me to admit that Harvard was number one) – and there are another forty-eight ranked above Newcastle. British applicants have begun to wake up to this reality. I am the second generation in my family to go to Harvard, but I am the first to find myself surrounded by Brits who have chosen the same track.

Many refuse even to consider the US option because they believe it is simply too expensive for them. But the rise of tuition fees in England is slowly forcing people to look across the Atlantic. The excellent financial aid and bursary programmes in place at most American universities ensure that many British students can afford to go, regardless of their educational background or economic status. The recent slide of the dollar puts living expenses within reach. Most students will graduate with less debt than their British contemporaries.

Not every part of the American educational system has been

wonderful. I have worked harder at Harvard than ever before in my life. I have undergone culture shock, missed my friends and family and developed an increasingly bizarre way of speaking. I have also made a dent in the bank balance of several very special people. But none of these obstacles would stand in my way if I had to choose my college path all over again. America has offered me something I could not find in England – a freedom to explore both academically and personally, and a chance to make friends with people whom I would never have met back home.

This book is designed to answer all the questions you might have about the American college system. It will tell you who to see, what to ask and when to do so. It looks at a selection of the many excellent schools and tries to give you an idea of what life would be like for you on the inside. But most of all, we hope, it will inspire you at least to consider the idea of America as you begin to make those nerve-wracking decisions about what you actually want from life.

About The Educational Advisory Service of the US–UK Fulbright Commission and Anthony Nemecek

Anthony Nemecek is the current Director of the US Educational Advisory Service (EAS) of the US–UK Fulbright Commission. Anthony has twenty years' experience working in educational settings in both the US and the UK. He has taught in schools and universities in the US and has worked in the FE and HE sectors in the UK in both lecturing and managerial positions, and has served as an assistant examiner for the Oxford, Cambridge and RSA Examinations Board.

EAS is the only official and independent source of information on US education in the UK. It provides objective, accurate and comprehensive information and advice to individuals and organizations. EAS does not endorse or rank any college or university, nor does it endorse services provided by any individual, company or organization. Its main reference library in London holds undergraduate and postgraduate guides, financial directories, university prospectuses and test preparation bulletins and books. Additional regional and secondary centres supported by EAS, across the UK hold a selection of guides and directories. See the Reference Section for details.

US Educational Advisory Service
US–UK Fulbright Commission
62 Doughty Street
London
WC1N 2JZ
Tel: 020 7404 6994
Fax: 020 7404 6994
Website: *www.fulbright.co.uk*

About *The Good Schools Guide*

If you are looking at choosing a university, then *The Good Schools Guide* is one book you don't need. We need your help, though. Tell us about the schools that have given you the education and ambition to try for a US university.

The Good Schools Guide was founded in 1985 by two parents in search of schools for their children. Nineteen years later there are almost fifty of us, spread throughout the UK. Most are parents with young children; a few are former heads and senior teachers.

We view schools from a parent's point of view, and choose schools for the Guide on the basis of what parents and pupils say about them. We define good schools as schools that are good for the children and parents they serve, and are not influenced by academic results alone.

If you think that one of the schools you attended should be recommended to others, go to *www.goodschoolsguide.co.uk*, navigate to the page for that school, and click on 'Enter your comments about this school'.

Contribute to *Uni in the USA*

This book would not exist without the thoughts, experiences and ideas of the British students who have trekked their way across the Atlantic and told us what they thought. Hopefully this is the first edition of a long line that will smooth the way for others who are heading West. But we need your comments, your corrections and your advice if we are to continue to do a good job. Please contact us at:

www.uniintheusa.com
Editor@uniintheusa.com
Or at 3 Craven Mews, London SW11 5PW

Foreword

The wisdom I inherited from my own school days of the 1960s and from my early days of school teaching was that a Brit should take his first degree in the UK and, if he felt so inclined, embark on post-graduate work, be it a Master's or an MBA, across the Atlantic. The arguments in favour of such a course remain valid: the A level curriculum is geared towards higher education in the UK, admissions tutors understand such a background, the transition from school to college curriculum ought to be straightforward, the cost is predictable. Yet in each of these areas there is change and the arguments carry less force than they did.

A level is not as dominant as it was. British universities are becoming more familiar with International Baccalaureate (IB) candidates and those from other routes including overseas students. Tomlinson is introducing further changes which tend towards greater breadth and postponed specialization; add to this the political controversy about maintained school quotas and the consequent insecurity engendered by fear of discrimination against the independent sector, and application to American universities begins to look more attractive, either as a back-up to UCAS or as a substitute.

The differential in cost is also being reduced, partly through the introduction of tuition fees with the parallel reduction in government grants and loans, and partly through the significant recent strengthening of the pound against the dollar.

American degree courses have always had advantages. They offer a wide choice of combined units, particularly but not exclusively in the first two years. The major degree subject does not have to be identified initially and indeed in professional areas such as medicine the final decision comes only at postgraduate level. How often I have heard pupils entering the Sixth Form complain that they are not ready to narrow their range of subjects, declaring that they have no firm idea of a future career path! There is little doubt that the four years at an American college bring a fuller educational experience with greater cultural and social coherence, combined with outstanding athletic facilities, especially at colleges like Stanford, Princeton or Duke where the campus is self-contained and focused. If, as seems likely, educational reform in Britain continues to enhance breadth, flexibility, the postponement of career decisions and the extension of education and training well beyond the three years of a first degree, the American model will appear prophetic and that tradition refined through the experience of many decades will be even more widely respected.

Against the positive attractions must be weighed what may prove to be the negative factors. This book addresses practical issues, including the social and cultural challenges. For the majority, college life is the first experience of living away from home and the transition may come as a shock. It stands to reason that those who will find the adjustment difficult will find it all the more so at 3,000+ miles and a whole culture apart. How quickly will you make the journey through Trifonovitch's four stages of cultural adjustment (see page 15)? Routines and learning styles, work assignments and seminars also introduce a new world. To whom will you turn for help when you feel at sea? Are you resilient, self-confident, resourceful?

So, to take the plunge or not? You will make your own decision, but there is a wealth of useful information in the pages which follow. What I can say without hesitation is that very few, if any, of those British pupils whom I have seen make their way to American universities have regretted their decision. I can also add confidently that the twelve young American graduates whom I saw in action as supernumerary short-term teachers at St Paul's, joining us immediately after their first degree and with no formal teaching qualification, brought the fruits of a very fine education which combined breadth and depth, enabling science majors to teach philosophy and ethics, historians to teach courses on film or theatre, English majors to conduct seminars on political theory. The richness, diversity and personal charisma of these 'Colet Fellows' were a tribute to their own university experience, an experience open to students embarking on degree courses from schools in the UK and arguably more appropriate for them than ever before.

If financial considerations can be set aside, the choice between the UK and the USA is a close one. The 'safer' option is to recognize the excellence of so many British universities and to take the UCAS route; the more adventurous and for some the more fulfilling route will be to look further West. If you have the personal confidence and a healthy dose of independence, if you value breadth at the outset, if you are undaunted by hard work and regular grade assessments, if what you know of American life attracts you, then go for it!

Stephen Baldock, High Master,
St Paul's School, London (1992–2004)

Some Useful Background Info

Making the decision to apply to a US university for your undergraduate course can be exciting if a bit daunting. There are over 4,000 colleges and universities in the US, of which approximately 2,000 offer undergraduate degrees (four years). You will be in good company: between the 2002/3 and 2003/4 academic years, the US Educational Advisory Service (EAS) in London has seen enquiries and website visits rise sevenfold (to 350,000) and has spoken to more people two months into this academic year than in the whole of the previous year. There are already over 8,000 UK students taking higher education in the United States.

Dealing With the Terminology

Learning how Americans define their universities is an important part of the application process. Failure to suss the semantics can land you in trouble! For example, rather than referring to the delights of your 'uni', you will constantly be talking about your 'school', causing some confusion among grandparents who thought you had passed your A levels. Here we explain some of the terminology of the US university system (and, in case you're wondering, university is used interchangeably with both school and college!).

Accreditation

Accreditation has to be your biggest consideration when looking at US universities, not only to ease credit transfer, but to ensure recognition of your degree when you come back to the UK. It is vital to make sure that your university is accredited by a body recognized by the Council for Higher Education Accreditation (CHEA) in Washington, DC. If the school or university is not accredited by one of these agencies, there may be problems with recognition and acceptance of your qualification both within the US and in the UK.

The Ivy League

(HARVARD, PRINCETON, YALE, BROWN, COLUMBIA, PENN, DARTMOUTH, CORNELL)

The Ivy League schools are the Holy Grail of the US college admissions process – the American equivalent of Oxbridge. But while these elite colleges enjoy some of the best reputations in America, the famous title actually started out as little more than the name of a sports division (and not even a particularly good one). No one, however, dares dispute the academic excellence of the Ivies. Each school is remarkably different, but all are situated on the East Coast and all enjoy stellar reputations. Ivy League graduates are at the top of the tree in finance, media and politics (among other areas), and most of them never shut up about how it was their glory years in the most prestigious colleges that got them where they are today. In fact, there is a plethora of universities in America that more than rival the Ivy League, but society finds it hard to resist that old East Coast arrogance and these colleges remain among the most popular (and most difficult to get into).

Liberal Arts Colleges

Many US universities claim to follow a liberal arts curriculum, but few can actually label themselves liberal arts colleges. This epithet applies only to a select group of mostly superb schools that pride themselves on the instruction of the undergraduate. As a result, they tend to have smaller campuses and fewer irritating grad students hanging around stealing the professors' attention.

Liberal arts programmes are designed to give you a broad and basic education rather than prepare you for a professional career. As a result you will normally be expected to come up to scratch in a range of academic disciplines. This ensures that, at the end of four years, you emerge as a well-rounded individual. Most liberal arts colleges are private schools, and Williams, Amherst and Swarthmore are normally recognized as the top three options. But students who want the breadth of a variety of courses need not confine their search to those colleges that are officially 'liberal arts'. The majority of undergraduate programmes at good universities insist their students take a broad base of courses.

Public Schools/State Universities

Don't get confused! When you hear someone refer to a public school, they don't mean the Eton and Harrow equivalents of America but rather the institutions that are supported by the state and open to all members of the public (which actually makes more sense if you think about it). These schools have names like Penn State or the University of Indiana and the majority of the student body hails from within that state, something that allows them to pay reduced fees. Public/state universities tend to be huge in size and some of them are absolutely excellent (UCLA and UVA). Be warned, though – standards vary immensely and, if you are an out-of-state candidate, competition is generally fierce.

State vs Private Universities – Which Come Cheaper?

In the United States, private universities make up 75% of all institutions. However, 75% of US students attend the remaining 25% – the state universities. State universities are founded and subsidized by state governments to provide a lower cost higher education to residents of their state. With student bodies of 20,000 plus, they admit a wider range of students than private universities. For UK students, the economic incentive that US students have for attending their 'state' university unfortunately does not exist. For example, if a resident of Ohio attends Ohio State University, their fees will be much lower than those of anyone who lives out of state. However, the fees for non-residents, while much higher, are still less than private university fees. Unfortunately, there will be little, if any, financial aid available to international students.

Private universities are funded by a combination of fees, grants, endowments and gifts from alumni. They are usually much smaller and, as a result, are much harder to get into. They are also far more likely to be able to provide financial assistance to international students.

Community Colleges

Another option, and one which may be appealing for both late developers and those struggling economically, is the community college. Community colleges, also known as junior colleges, are similar to the FE sector in the UK. They provide two-year courses leading to an associate's degree – very similar to an HND. As a rule, admissions criteria are much more flexible, many not even requiring an admissions test such as the SAT. They are also much, much cheaper and thus attractive to those on a tight budget.

Many students elect to attend a community college for the first two years of their degree and then transfer to a four-year institution, similar to topping up an HND. In fact, many community colleges have agreements with prestigious universities that successful completion of their course will guarantee acceptance. For students who, perhaps, have not yet proved themselves academically, the community college route offers an opportunity to demonstrate their capabilities and save a lot of money. For some international students, the community college may make the transition to the American system more comfortable, as a more gradual means of acclimatizing to the American style of assessment, etc.

The downside to community colleges is that they tend to attract older students, and it may be more difficult to find a satisfying social group. They also may not have the resources to provide special support for international students, and may not offer the total 'living' experience provided by four-year institutions – many do not cater for housing, etc. If you are considering a community college, find out what agreements they have with four-year institutions and what sort of support they offer international students, both academically and socially, before you make any decisions.

What's an American University Education Really Like?

The greatest difference between Bachelor degrees in the US and BAs in the UK is summed up by two words: 'liberal' and 'arts'. If you feel that nothing but three years of physics is right for you, then stay at home. If you know what you're good at but want to explore a hundred other things as well, then the US may be just what you need. Have no idea? Head to America and put off those daunting decisions for a little while longer. Students at a liberal arts college or a university with a strong liberal arts programme – most of the ones covered in this guide – can take classes in a wide variety of courses before zeroing in on a specialist subject. Even if you plan to major in engineering, you will usually have to take courses in the humanities and social sciences, while history majors will be required to undertake courses in maths and science subjects. The end result? A flexible education that enables you to carry on exploring academically throughout your undergraduate career.

This philosophy is one of the most striking differences between UK and US degree programmes. For some students the thought of having to take a subject that they may have gratefully left behind at GCSE level will be unappealing, but the US system believes in urging everyone to explore a varied curriculum before committing themselves to a major area of focus.

This system also makes the US degree far more flexible for those students who are unable to make up their minds. For the most part, any class (or course in American lingo) taken to fulfil the liberal arts core can also be used to fulfil graduation requirements. It is thus perfectly possible to start out as a history major and change to Spanish, without losing any time. What is more, should you decide to transfer to a different university, you can bring what you have already completed with you – rather than having to start over. Obviously, there will be instances when you cannot transfer directly because courses will differ from university to university, but for the most part universities are co-operative and accept transfer credits.

There's plenty of single-minded education on offer in the US too – though the best of it is often postgraduate only. Large universities tend to comprise colleges of arts and sciences and several 'professional' – i.e. career-oriented – schools, such as business, agriculture, medicine, law and journalism. Institutes of technology have a scientific emphasis.

Tinker, Tailor, Doctor, Lawyer

If you are one of those noble characters who has known from the cradle that you have a vocation for mending broken bodies or diagnosing ingrowing toenails, then you may regard the American medical school system as a serious waste of time. There are hardly any courses for undergraduates seeking a medical degree in the United States (with the exception of a couple, such as the combined courses at Northwestern). Instead, would-be doctors must go through their college career as pre-meds, combining the courses that will set them on track to med school with those that give them a liberal arts education.

Though frustrating for many, this approach does guarantee a wider base of knowledge and means that you are not exposed to the gore and pressure of the medical system at the tender age of eighteen. But being a pre-med is no easy task. The requirements are fairly painful and, if you plan to carry on in the US system, you will have to take your MCATs while studying for your undergrad degree. This dreaded nine-hour exam is a multiple choice stamina test that is mandatory for entry into the many excellent American medical schools. The advantage of this system is that, if you are presently considering medicine as a career option, but are by no means set on it, you get an extra three years of broad education while you make up your mind. The disadvantage is that pre-meds work harder than most other students and still have to jump through the extra hoop of applications at the end of the four years.

Even then, you are chancing your arm if you intend to stay on in the US for your postgraduate medical studies. Fewer than one-half of 1% of students in US medical colleges are international students. Therefore, even if you hold an appropriate undergraduate degree, the likelihood of acceptance is virtually nil. Those still set on a US medical education should be aware that, once you have completed your medical studies in the UK, it is quite possible to enter the US for your residency/clinical practice stage. Contact the US

Educational Advisory Service for additional information.

Would-be lawyers in America find themselves in a similar situation. There is no actual undergraduate law degree. Instead, the students designate themselves (you've guessed it) pre-laws and round off their college career with the LSATs. Those set on a legal career do not have the same college-imposed requirements as their medical peers, but they do have to suffer the slings and arrows of important grad school applications and tests in the midst of what should be the final fun fling of their collegiate years.

For students wanting to study law, the prospects of graduate study in the US after earning an LLB in the UK are bright. If it is your goal to practise law in the US, following your LLB, you can apply to do a one-year LLM (Master's in Law) in the US and may be able to take the qualifying bar exam in several states. As each state sets its own requirements, and they change frequently, it is best to consult with the EAS first.

The Facts of the Matter

An American education is hard work. Your friends back home will spend much of their first year sitting in the pub while you spend it trekking backwards and forwards from the library. The fact that most of these universities operate under the principle of continuous assessment means that goofing off for semesters at a time is not an option. Instead, practically everything you do in a class will influence the eventual status of your degree. Exams (usually at least two per term), tests (sometimes unannounced), essays or written assignments, problem sets, laboratory reports, laboratory practicals, class attendance and discussion participation may all be used to determine your final grade. While you get a chance to laugh at the Brits back home when they all start panicking about finals, you will have spent four years working much harder than them on a day-to-day basis.

US colleges do not come cheaply and you should expect to get your money's worth in terms of hours of class. There's none of that 'six hours of tuition a week, attendance optional if you have a hangover' stuff here. Students should expect to attend at least twelve hours of lectures a week with quality professors. Attendance at several smaller sessions (something akin to tutorials) with graduate students will also be required. And falling behind on that massive reading load really isn't a possibility if you hope to keep those grades up. Courses are marked as a percentage, then translated to the letter grade scale as follows (with some minor variations): 100–90% = A; 89–80% = B; 79–70% = C; 69–60% = D; 59–50% = E = Fail. Other systems stretch to F for fail. Competition for those A grades tends to be fierce, so prepare yourself for four years of hard work.

There is one easier option available to the lazier variety of student. This is to take a course on a pass/fail basis rather than for a letter grade. Most universities have become wise to this easy out, however, and there may well be a limit to the number of courses a student may take by this method. The option also may not be available if the course is required for the student's major. The system works well, however, for students who want to experiment in different fields but don't want a potentially low grade to risk their treasured GPA (see below).

However hard you work, you can rest assured you are not the only person putting in long hours. While America expects a lot from its students, it also expects its professors to teach well. Students are able to assess their lecturers' performance at the end of each course, and access to members of the faculty is generally less restricted than in England. America prides itself on the unity of its academic communities, and professors are normally fairly involved in undergraduate education. But don't be a shy and retiring Brit about it. US students have been trained from an early age to go out there and introduce themselves to that scary person lecturing at you. Learn to do likewise and you will benefit hugely.

The Credit System

American undergraduate degrees allow you a variety of options. Students usually experience a wide variety of courses before selecting a major upon which to focus. It is also possible to create your own unique programme of study. Every course you take each semester earns a specified number of credits (also termed hours and units). You get your degree when you have completed the appropriate number of credits (normally after four years of full-time study). Don't worry, though – most US colleges have an advising system in place that allows students to discuss the courses they will take during the academic year with a tutor. This ensures that nothing vital gets overlooked.

It is not uncommon for students to take longer than four years to complete their degrees. This often happens if they take less than a full-time course load per term owing to academic or financial reasons. Students can also adjust their workloads between terms – taking five courses in one semester and only three in the next. Courses taken in the first two years are known as lower division courses and those in the final two years as upper division courses.

The individual courses that make up the degree programme can be divided into the following types:

Core courses These provide the centre of the degree programme. Students take a variety of courses drawn from maths, English, humanities, sciences, social sciences, foreign languages and foreign cultures. Core requirements vary from college to college but are the base of the liberal arts spirit and a valuable part of the American system.

Major courses A major is the subject upon which a student chooses to concentrate. Most students major in one subject, but some colleges offer the option of pursuing a double major with a related subject. Of the total number of courses required for the completion of a degree, one-quarter to one-half will be spent collecting credits for your major.

Minor courses A minor is a subject in which a student may choose to take the second greatest cluster of courses. The number of courses required for a minor tends to be half the number of major courses. Minors are a great way of pursuing a secondary interest, in such fields as languages or the arts.

Elective courses These courses may be chosen from any department and often have little to do with a student's major. They help make up the total number of credits required to graduate and also offer the student the chance really to explore everything their university has to offer. As a result, they can be one of the most fun parts of an American degree.

What Is a GPA?

Instead of a degree classification, students complete their degree with a Grade Point Average (GPA). A cumulative Grade Point Average is the GPA for all courses taken throughout the degree programme. This number is what prospective employers look at, and during the job-hunting season you will see your classmates frantically trying to calculate their total.

To work out your GPA, you assign a numerical value to each letter grade you achieved (most universities use 4 for an A, 3 for a B and so on, but a few, purely to confuse, score an A as five and so on down). You then multiply this number by the number of credits the course is worth to give total grade points for the course. Add all these up and divide by the total number of credits for all the courses you have taken – hey presto, there's your average grade points per credit – your GPA.

Most universities will also offer some sort of honours degree (in the UK this comes free with the BA, like an Oxbridge MA). To qualify for an honours degree you must acquire additional credits or write an honours thesis. Precise details depend on the university and/or academic department, so make sure you find out about it early in your college career. There may well be different levels of honours: summa cum laude, magna cum laude and cum laude, in descending order of distinction, based on your GPA and the honours extras.

The Academic Calendar

The academic year will be slightly different for each university/college but will normally run from early September to the end of May. It may be divided into two terms of eighteen weeks called 'semesters', or the university may have 'quarters' or 'trimesters' which are about twelve weeks in length. Additionally, universities often provide six to eight-week summer terms, but these are optional. Many students attend if they wish to decrease their course load during the regular terms, or simply make up for lost ground. There are at least two main holidays during the academic year: a two to four-week break over Christmas and a one-week Spring Break somewhere between early March and mid-April.

English students should, however, beware. America offers none of the three long holidays a year system that so many British schools enjoy. The Christmas break is fairly short and Easter does not exist. The one-week Spring Break, which college students treat as a big excuse for drunkenness and debauchery, can leave you more exhausted than relaxed, and the haul from January to May is a long one. American summer holidays are huge but most of your contemporaries will be using them for work experience. Relaxation does not figure largely in the American calendar – occasional breaks for President's Day or Thanksgiving are the most time off you can really expect in the academic year – something to bear in mind if you are someone who enjoys leisure time.

Money, Money, Money

America might proclaim itself the 'land of the free', but there is no getting around the fact that an American education is anything but. Tuition fees in Britain look lightweight alongside the hefty cheques that American parents are forced to pay out for their children's education. Sadly, the exorbitant cost of a good American college is enough to dissuade most Brits from even considering the option. Don't be downhearted! It is a frequently held misconception that all international students at an American college come equipped with their own million-dollar trust fund. This is miles from the truth. A first-rate education abroad is becoming an ever more achievable option for British students of all backgrounds.

One of the reasons American universities have thrived is their remarkable management of financial resources. Universities like Harvard have bank balances that rival the largest American corporations and exceed those of many a developing country. Alumni from all over the nation pour money back into their alma maters, and boards of savvy businessmen make sure their colleges are never short of funds. All this financial acumen allows for the generous subsidies and financial aid packages that enable students from even the most disadvantaged backgrounds to attend the college of their dreams.

The sum total ...

Tuition and fees are usually based on a nine-month academic year that runs from September to May. Tuition is the charge for instruction, while fees tend to cover services such as use of the library and student health service. The total costs will vary greatly, from $4,000 to $50,000 per academic year (the average is $18,000).

Books/supply costs, travel costs and other personal expenses such as health insurance also need to be added in. American universities require students to purchase a lot of textbooks and these can be expensive. It is not unusual to have a book bill of $200–400 per semester.

And then there's the cost of life on campus. Obviously, this will vary depending on location and personal lifestyle, but most universities publish guidelines in the $5,000–12,000 range. In places such as New York and Boston, living on baked beans may be your only option to keep within budget.

And how to deal with it ...

Brits at university in the US do not have the LEA option of a student loan. In the long-term this is a great benefit, leaving you debt-free once you're out in the real world. In the short-term, though, you are deprived of the chance of blowing all your money in the pub (if they had pubs), or on that cute pair of shoes, then living hand-to-mouth for the rest of the year. You will be living hand-to-mouth all year round anyway.

One solution is to get a job – though many find this hard to fit into their pressured academic schedule. Another is to negotiate with your parents before the start of the academic year and agree on a loan with them – one that can be adjusted in either direction once you have gauged just how expensive campus life really is.

The main source of financial assistance for UK students, after family contributions, will be the university itself. Many, but not all, give help to international students. During the application process, you will have to submit information that will enable the university to assess your family's financial situation. They then work out how much they can reasonably be expected to contribute to the cost of your education. Many US universities will not charge you more than that amount. For example, if the university reckons the family contribution ought to be £200 a year – that is all you will have to pay for your tuition and fees. Not all universities are so generous, but you will be surprised how many are!

And for the athletes among you, there's always the option of a sports scholarship (see p. 227).

Grants

A grant is the sum a university gives towards the cost of your education. A grant may also cover living expenses, depending on your circumstances, but it is unlikely because they are usually given on the basis of merit rather than need.

Loans

Some universities offer international student loans. It may also be possible to arrange a loan in the UK before you go – rare, but not unheard of. Additionally, if you have a US citizen who would act as a co-signer, many US banks and financial companies will grant loans to international students. Just remember, if you do take this option, bang goes coming away from university debt-free.

Working on and off campus ...

Unlike the hallowed halls of Oxford and Cambridge where work of a non-academic or pint-lifting variety is all but outlawed, American universities positively encourage their students to work outside classes. The love affair with capitalism that has propelled America so far in the world is instilled at an early age, and the majority of your classmates will have been doing a paper round or working in shops for years. The expense of the American college system, and the stipulations of most financial aid plans, mean that many students need to find paid employment if they are to pay their way through school. The bad news is that, as an international student, you cannot just walk into any place with a 'Help Wanted' sign, do your shift and pick up a pay cheque. The good news is that your international visa allows you to work on campus (although not off) after you have applied for a social security card – in itself a lengthy and frustrating process. (NB: Earnings from this work cannot be counted as a source of income for official finance statements, see p. 209-10.) Once you've got your hands on one of these, you have the freedom to take whatever university job you can find and earn money for it legally. Most universities have an employment office that helps students to find work in the libraries, laboratories or administration of the college – jobs that are usually set aside just for students.

The real problems start if you want to work off-campus in the US through the summers. Many students aim to do this and, if you are one of them, then you need to plan ahead. Getting a job is a cinch in comparison with getting permission to take it. Some international students choose to do unpaid volunteering jobs or internships as a way round the problem. However, for those who need or want the money there are other, lengthier routes (aside from the illegal under-the-counter cash options).

As an international student you are allowed one year of Optional Practical Training (or OPT). This is permission, which has to be applied for, to work anywhere in the US for a stated amount of time. You can do anything, from waitressing to investment banking. Many students prefer to save up their OPT year for the end of their studies when they can spend a sizeable amount of time in the States. If you are planning to do this, you should be warned that your OPT year begins immediately after graduation. Others choose to use up a couple of months (the year does not have to be taken all at once) every summer. The great thing about OPT is that you have the flexibility to do what you want, when you want.

The official line is that permission for OPT will come through about a month after applying. Do NOT assume that the official line is true. The process takes forever. All applications are shipped to service stations in remote parts of the county where they dawdle indefinitely, finally getting to you after you should have already started work. Consult your international adviser on this, but really try to leave three months to get this permission through. The wheels of bureaucracy grind extremely slowly, when they grind at all.

There is another and much quicker option for some individuals. Curricular Practical Training (or CPT) allows you to find paid work anywhere as long as it is related to the subject you are studying. Best for those interested in sciences, medicine or technology where practical internships are plentiful, it is an option worthy of anyone's investigation. For the most part, professors are amenable to this and permission is fairly easy to obtain. CPT has no time limit and does not detract from your OPT allotment in any way.

Occasionally you can enrol in a class for the summer and get work permission that way. This depends very much on the attitudes of your professors and international office. As deadlines and requirements change on an annual basis, the best idea is to make an early appointment with your international adviser. Inevitably there is always some way to work through the system and get permission for doing paid work. It is just an arduous process.

Culture Shock

Love America one minute? Hate it the next? For students concerned about the normality of their reaction to American life, there is an answer. Sociologist Gregory Trifonovitch has studied the experiences of students transplanted to another culture and outlined the four stages of cultural adjustment. Below is the kind of experience you may encounter during your first few months in America.

The Honeymoon Stage Upon arrival, everything is wonderful. The Americans are so friendly, everyone loves your accent and the price of jeans in GAP is half that at home. You love your adopted country and it seems to love you. Until …

The Hostility Stage Suddenly everything is a little too strange. Where are your friends? Why is there no pub? What on earth are people talking about? This is the stage at which Trifonovitch believes most international students experience frustration and depression, due mostly to the difficulties of settling into a new environment. The tendency is to lash out at the new surroundings – think phone calls home outlining the stranger habits of the bloody Americans. This is the point at which you must make sure you are meeting lots of new people, developing those initial connections into real friendships and talking to friends or counsellors about any problems you are having.

The Humour Stage Suddenly one day you wake up and you know how to deal with being a Brit in America. Mistakes are no longer irritating. They are funny. Suddenly you like being the outsider.

The Home Stage Eventually you are a veteran. Despite your misgivings, you start defending American foreign policy to your English friends, in much the same way you defend the British Empire to your American ones. You have become culturally ambidextrous – a true transatlantic traveller.

A Shared History?

Everyone considering applying to a US university should understand that the experience will have its ups and its downs. There will be good friends who open your eyes to a whole new cultural awareness. And, yes, there will be bad times when you feel like banging your head against the wall and screaming, 'Get me out of here!'. Always, there will be the constant reminder that you are, in essence, different from these people.

It may be the evening when everyone gets drunk and decides to sing the theme tunes from their favourite childhood television shows. When you start to sing *Neighbours* or *Byker Grove*, they'll suddenly go blank and you'll shudderingly realize these English (or Australian) classics never quite made it across the pond. Or it may be the time you try and remind everyone about that great single that Ash released and the time you tried to sing it on a pub table after your GCSE results. Again, although there may be a few indulgent smiles, the vast majority of Americans will be sitting there thinking 'Poor crazy English kid'. The sad truth is that, no matter how assimilated you become, the trends, jokes and cultural history of your childhood and adolescence will always be a mystery to Americans. However, when you really think about it, how much of your time at college do you really want to spend discussing that romance in *Hollyoaks* or the names of all four Teletubbies?

Fellow Brits

At the majority of these universities you will discover a significant number of international undergraduates. In those first baffled days as you grapple with registration, visa snags and the mysteries of the American language, it is all too easy to fall in with those you most closely identify with – your fellow countrymen. After all, they share a common background, a similar accent and, given the minute scale of England, mutual geographical and social history. AND the chances are they're just as bemused by Americans as you are ...

These people can become your extended siblings – friends with whom to make sense of an alien environment and who can help you to assimilate. Just because you have decided to make the move out of England does not mean you should slam the door on all its other exports. To have a truly international university experience you need to foster your links with the past at the same time as embracing the future.

Yet it is also important you do not isolate yourself from the American community. If you are surrounded solely by Brits or Europeans from day one, it can be difficult to make contact with actual Americans – an integral part (unsurprisingly) of the American educational experience. The natives of your new country do not all share the same background and the chances are many of them will feel as lost as you. Getting to know roommates and class-mates who come from places you would never be able to pinpoint on a map is essential and the most rewarding thing you can do. Of course, there will always be Brits available to form an emergency support system but, at the vast majority of these colleges, they are an extremely small minority. Americans are the people who will come to form the major body of your friends, and, whatever your angst about accent or cultural background, you must turn to them from the beginning.

The Dating Game

Does absence make the heart grow fonder? The start of freshman year always sees a significant handful of loyal souls clinging to the relationships that have defined their teenage years. As the year progresses, however, many of these relationships fall by the wayside. Leaving a 'significant other' back home is not an easy trick to pull off. The social/drunken/hormonal atmosphere of university means the relationship will be severely tested and, even if the one drunken slip doesn't zap it, the mileage probably will. There is also the undeniably irritating, but also undeniably true, parental dictum – 'too serious, too young'. College is after all a time to get out there and try new things – so don't tie yourself down or you might end up resenting that one true love.

This is not to say that long-distance relationships don't work. After all, America has some pretty bizarre dating rituals and some people just feel more comfortable sticking to what they know. But it pays to consider the options before you swear eternal devotion and get on that plane. And if you do decide to stay together, for goodness sake invest in an international calling card and a beneficial air miles deal!

Braving the new

Remember those high-school movies? The ugly ducking turns into a swan, the jock discovers his heart, the whole thing comes together in one great romantic climax on prom night ...? American fact or Hollywood fiction? It's difficult to tell but, whatever the answer, one truth stands out – dating in the United States is a whole new experience.

Of course, as in England, it is difficult to generalize about relationships across the range of universities. Students who head for one of the more relaxed and less academic schools will discover dating scenarios that are totally different from the insanely introspective and esoteric relationships that define some of the Ivy Leagues. Think *Road Trip* versus *Love Story*. But there are some crucial elements to American romance that seem to go across the board.

First of all, there is the definition of the word 'dating'. In Britain its meaning is clear: you're going out. But in America you can quite easily be routinely seeing the same person, yet have absolutely no idea what the dating status of your relationship actually is. Let alone if it even has one! There comes a point when casual dating evolves into monogamous dating and it still isn't quite a relationship but doesn't allow relationships with anyone else but ... well, you get the idea. Americans seem to be born with an embedded cultural chip enabling them to understand all of this stuff, but Brits are frequently left bemused.

Second, the date itself is a somewhat different experience. This may be due to the alcohol restrictions in this country. Somehow inEngland, pubs, bars and clubs lend themselves to drunken encounters which sometimes develop into something more memorable. In America, however, the most used phrase is 'Let's have coffee'. It makes no difference if neither of you actually like coffee – the formalities have to be preserved. No wonder Starbucks is so popular!

Even getting to the coffee stage is something to be proud of. Forget any rules of relationships you may have learnt at home. Do not expect to go on dates alone – everyone continues to travel as a pack. Do not expect the man to call on day three. American men are used to more aggressive women. (Although, if you are the kind of girl who has a little Old World reticence, rest assured it could work to your advantage!) And if you get stuck – for goodness sake, ask an American, not an international student, for advice.

Perhaps the whole debacle can best be summed up in the words of a frustrated friend who studied in America (capitals her own): 'The "dating" KILLED ME. What I really like about European guys is they tend to tell you whether they like you or not. Then I came to

North Carolina and went on a date with this guy. The movie ended and he drove me home. Nothing happened. Then he didn't call again for about a week. Then we went out to dinner and to the beach. Then he drove me home. STILL nothing happened. Then he didn't call for a few days. Then we went out again ... AND THIS WENT ON FOR A MONTH OR TWO ... I didn't know how to deal with the whole situation any longer so I got him drunk and ONLY THEN something happened ... and all the other girls from America were telling me not to stress as nothing seemed wrong!!! But HOW CAN SOMEONE KIND OF BE YOUR BOYFRIEND?! HE IS EITHER YOUR BOYFRIEND OR HE IS NOT YOUR BOYFRIEND'.

And for the boys ...

British boys have one secret weapon in their mission to conquer the fair daughters of America – their accent. It is undeniably true that when English men open their mouths, American girls swoon. (Girls, you can also work your 'cute' accent to your advantage, but don't be prepared for quite the same effect.) It may have something to do with Prince William, but the average Yankee girl will initially seem more than receptive to your suave English charm. So all of your dreams about the liberated American woman, sun-kissed, schooled in the arts of high-school seduction and just waiting for her own personal Prince Charming may very well come true. Certainly, Brits who come to visit US college campuses can be heard uttering resounding cries of 'American girls are SO fit!'. (Note: don't offer this as a compliment here – no one will have any idea what you're talking about.)

However, it is only fair to point out that many British boys have noted a down side to this liberated American female. She has, for the most part, been brought up to believe that it pays to take a more aggressive attitude towards dating. Women are not backward about coming forward on college campuses (probably because they have to make a stand just to cut through the American boy's deeply relaxed attitude). The straightforward nature of the American girl can be great. You know that she likes you, she singles you out, it's good for your ego. At the same time, many English gentlemen begin to feel they are losing control. After all, they have been taught it is polite to hold open doors and pay for meals. Ultimately, however, these differences seem to work themselves out – and the long tradition of young American girls falling in love with distinguished English gents suggests you may well be in with a chance of enjoying a functional relationship on the other side of the Atlantic!

Fraternities

When you tell your British friends you are planning on attending an American university, it is more than likely that at least one of them will look at you with pity and mutter something disparaging about fraternities. These Greek societies have been much parodied in Hollywood movies, most famously in the iconic *Animal House*, and remain the thing most Brits commonly associate with US universities. And while the majority of American college girls do not live in sororities that specialize in naked pillow-fights and most American boys do not swallow goldfish as part of their pledge routines, the Greek system is still alive and kicking on a large number of American campuses.

These social groups (often named after random Greek letters – Kappa Kappa Delta, and so on) are particularly dominant in Southern and state universities, but exist across the United States. On many campuses, they form an integral part of the social life, offering the students privately owned buildings where it is possible to party (and drink) in relative peace. They also offer alternative accommodation to the university dorms for their members. Although some of them remain hugely secretive and exclusive, the majority of universities have insisted that any Greek house on campus must open its doors to all students. As a result, frats and sororities have become much more integrated into college life than they used to be (and certainly much more so than the mysterious secret societies at Yale and UVA).

Scandals do, however, continue to hang over these Greek institutions. Accusations of sexual assault, drunken casualties and the 'hazing' that takes place during rush and initiation seasons (when the frats are recruiting more members) are rife. As far as you are concerned, most of the schools mentioned in this guide are not dominated by the Greek institutions (although the majority have active chapters on campus), and nowadays most college students find their social life extends in other directions. However, if you are bent on being the next Iota Gamma, it pays to do your research before signing away your life. After all, you don't want to become the next John Belushi.

Pubs and Prohibition

The majority of Brits spend their college days enveloped in a haze of alcohol that oils the wheels of their social lives, cushions their academic crises and whips up their weekends, weeks, evenings and even the odd morning. Not so their American neighbours. In the good old US of A you can use a shotgun almost as soon as you can carry it, drive a car from the age of 16 and kill for your country before you even consider university. Yet, until your twenty-first birthday, a glass of wine with dinner or a pint of beer at a football game remains a cr crminal offence.

Almost all American students think this rule ridiculous and all Europeans certainly do. Yet it remains and its effects are widely felt. Not only is it an impediment to normal socializing, it also means that far more importance is attached, in the freshman year particularly, to underage drinking. This can be disturbing for Brits who suddenly feel fourteen again, hiding their vodka bottles under the bed.

Fake IDs are the name of the game, and the majority of students turn to these to lubricate their first couple of years. Those lucky enough to have older brothers or sisters often nab their IDs. Be warned, however. Arrests happen frequently enough for actual concern, and there are horror stories among international students of offenders being deported. They are probably fictitious but it is certainly not uncommon for IDs to be confiscated and even handed to the police.

Of-age Brits should also be aware that their English driving licence is not considered by many of the more pedantic East Coast bartenders to be a sufficient form of identification. It pays to have a colour photocopy of your passport with you at all times. This also helps to clear up the issues of reversed dates (that whole month/day, day/month thing can be a nightmare).

Certain areas are infinitely more difficult than others. Unsurprisingly, Puritan New England suffers the most. In some areas (most notably Massachusetts) it is still illegal to buy alcohol on Sundays, and dry towns (a concept that would appal the average Englishman) are not uncommon. Those interested in hitting the biggest nightspot of them all will be relieved to learn that the majority of bars in New York City are considerably more relaxed.

No Smoking Please

It is easy to spot the Europeans on winter nights at East Coast American universities. While everyone else is tucked up in their dorm rooms, watching four feet of snow pile up around the windows, the Europeans are sitting on their doorsteps, shivering in an inadequate coat, and frantically trying to warm themselves by the heat of a much needed cigarette. They can only find this nicotine solace outdoors because recent legislation across most of the United States has banned smoking in restaurants, bars and clubs (as well as the more obvious offices and dorm rooms). Americans, particularly those of the educated variety, are frequently militant anti-smokers and, for Brits with a pack-a-day mentality, this can come as a rude surprise.

Certain areas of the States are much more draconian than others – in California, for example, the only cigarettes you are likely to come across are those chain-smoked by the odd Hollywood actress in a bid to expunge all food from her diet. But, although America as a whole is rapidly becoming a no-cigarette zone, stressed-out students are one sector of the population who can be relied upon to boost sales. Smoking comrades are always around, but the problem lies in finding somewhere to do it. And, for those of you who are die-hard smokers, two words of warning. First, the brainwashing power of American disapproval may be so strong you find yourself overwhelmed by the fug of smoke in English pubs when you come home for the holidays. Second, calling a cigarette a 'fag' is NOT a good idea unless you are given to provoking multiple misunderstandings, embarrassment and lectures on political correctness! (In the US, the *only* meaning for 'fag' is that of a male homosexual.)

Just Don't Inhale – and You Too Can Become President

Drug-taking among university students in America is really little different from drug-taking among their contemporaries in England. Some do it all the time, some never touch the stuff. The range of drugs is also pretty similar – rich, spoilt kids do cocaine, everyone else smokes pot, and the experimental ones swallow any pill going. If there is one small difference, it is the fact that marijuana is probably even more popular among students in the US than it is in the UK. The reason for this is probably because alcohol is so much harder to come by for under-21s in America, and it is often easier to smoke a joint in your dorm room than be chucked out by bar after bar on a Saturday night. Since the joys of Woodstock and the Swinging Sixties, pot has never really relinquished its place as drug of choice for students eager to escape reality.

However, this is not to say the American bureaucracy is willing to overlook a bunch of stoned students. Drug laws can be pretty tough, and, in case you need reminding, as an international student you are particularly liable for harsh punishment. Universities are normally willing to turn a blind eye to the first minor drug offence, but, as with alcohol, if you are going to indulge, you need to keep your wits about you and be careful not to get caught. Also, if you are a sportsman or going through the recruiting process for all those moneymaking finance jobs, you should be warned that random drug-testing is one of the perils of the process and something that has succeeded in dashing the hopes of many an ambitious stoner.

Workout Nation

Many Americans like to say their nation is fat in the middle and thin around the edges. This is certainly a country of extremes, and personal health is most definitely one of them. International students are frequently shocked by the sheer volume of food that people consume in the US. Movie shows come with a bucket of drink and a barrel of popcorn and even the nicer restaurants will slap half a cow on your plate and call it a steak. While obesity is a humungous problem in Middle America, college students normally need only worry about the dreaded 'freshman fifteen' (the fifteen pounds – read one stone plus – all students are rumoured to gain in their first year).

Once your mind and stomach have grown accustomed to the size of your plate, you will notice another thing – American students are obsessed with working out. It rivals only their dating rituals for most baffling personality trait. While students also play all the sports English universities do, they continue to regard the gym as a sort of second home. Jogging to them is like oxygen. You may well become sucked into this lifestyle – in fact, it may become the compensation for the size of your meals. But be warned, if you are one of the brave souls who manage to withstand the onslaught of comments about your lack of gym attendance, you will be marked down as slightly unnatural. After all, doesn't everyone want to run eight miles a day?

Cold Hard Cash

As far as banking practicalities go, never put your faith in the effectiveness of international monetary transactions. Although English bank cards work in most American ATMs, there is no point in draining your Lloyds account, incurring extra charges and constantly having to calculate the dollars/pounds exchange. By far the best option is to set up an American bank account. As students return to school, all the banks compete to offer the best possible options, and it is easy to get a good deal. Getting an American credit card is important too, especially for those who plan to stay on in the United States. Building up a credit history will help you later when you need to start paying for that mortgage or car.

Plus, if you are transferring large sums of money (or cheques) between countries, make sure you give it plenty of time. Banks often impose long waiting periods before they clear cheques, and this could prove catastrophic if your rent is due the next day!

Finally, a couple of other financial points. America is a nation that expects heavy tipping (to compensate for its remarkably low minimum wage). If you are paying for dinner or taking a taxi, leaving around 20% is considered normal. The traditional Brit who tips at 10% is treated with considerable disdain and won't necessarily be welcomed back.

And for those of you who are struggling with all those coins – here's a breakdown: 1 dollar = 100 cents; 1 quarter = 25 cents (the big coins, like the 10p and with fun state facts on them!); 1 dime = 10 cents (this is really confusing, they're the small ones – like 5p pieces); 1 nickel = 5 cents (bigger than the dime but less valuable!); 1 penny = 1 cent (borrowed from the English).

Hitting the Road

You're in the States. An open road in the land of opportunity stretches before you. A small piece of advice: get on it.

It is all too easy to downsize to your own little campus and spend four years languishing in an obscure corner of New England, Chicago or California. This familiar haven in a terrifyingly VAST land (that actually boasts ranches the size of England) will always feel like a secure American home for you. Don't let it trap you. Presumably you chose to come to the States because you have either some sort of wanderlust or a sense of adventure (or, in the worst case scenario, a real hatred of the UK). Going to university in such a unique environment should not kill your travel itch. Give it free rein and make all your British friends truly jealous.

Your travels are made that much easier by the fact that your American friends will be falling over themselves to show you around their hometowns. The colleges in this book are not only popular with international students, they also take Americans from all corners of the fifty states. Unless you select your friends using geographical criteria, the chances are that you will end up knowing people 'from California to the New York Island'. And on such random American holidays as Thanksgiving, the great American hospitality kicks in for the poor abandoned Brit. Accept all invitations, exploit all the long weekends you get and break out into as many of the fifty states as you possibly can.

The road trip remains a remarkable part of the American youth experience and one highly recommended to any Brit who can jump on board. If you have a friend with a car, you're set. The sole problem lies with your own driving. Not only do you face the challenges of driving on the wrong side of the road, you will also probably find you are too young to hire a car. If you fail totally in chartering your own set of wheels, the ubiquitous Greyhound (and numerous other) bus systems are more than adequate for the intrepid traveller.

Choosing a University

Selecting a university that is thousands of miles away, perhaps without the opportunity to visit beforehand, will worry even the most enthusiastic. Fortunately, thanks to the Internet and its assiduous use by US universities and students, you can get a good feel for an institution without adding to Branson's millions. Many universities provide virtual tours of their campuses and give you a clear description of student life and the services available to international students.

Just like in the UK, there are some key books to be thumbed over: see the Reference Section at the back of the book for a full list. Most of you will not need to buy any of them: the websites are stuffed with information and well laid out, and you can find the books at the US Educational Advisory Service libraries in Belfast, Birmingham, Dundee, Edinburgh, Glasgow, Hull, London, Londonderry, Manchester, Plymouth, St Andrews and Swansea (see the Reference Section for locations).

Additionally, many US university representatives visit the UK on a regular basis and attend the College Day USA fairs in London and Scotland which take place in early October. See *www.fulbright.co.uk/eas* for further information.

Academic Considerations

What is it you really want to study? If you have specific requirements, will the university you are looking at be able to satisfy your needs? US universities are often pretty flexible – many will allow you to design your own course within the academic resources they offer. But can you handle the requirements that they do have? Investigate. If you plan on studying a field that will have a professional examination or required affiliation once you return to the UK, ask the UK professional body how the US degrees you are looking at will be viewed. For the most part there are few problems, but you may be required to take additional coursework or sit an examination, and it is best to know this in advance.

How will a US university view your UK qualifications? Each in its own way (some of them have been reading our newspapers decrying the value of A levels, and may need some persuasion). Most, however, will give you credit for your A levels which can then be used to decrease the length of time needed to complete the degree. Many UK students find that an entire year can be 'waived' in this way. However, as each US university is entitled to set its own policies on credits awarded, it should be investigated before you apply.

Because there is such variety among US universities, it is essential, when looking for an appropriate institution, that you consider the difficulty of gaining admission. All universities will publish their general criteria. Look at that information carefully. You don't want to spend the time and money applying if your chances of getting in are hopeless. While US universities are extremely flexible and will look at each student individually, if your qualifications, SAT results, etc. are a long way off what they normally want, the likelihood is that you won't get in. However, with so many accredited universities from which to choose, there is almost certainly a university out there that will be the right match for you!

And how is the university you are looking at rated? Unlike the UK, there is no official ranking system in the US. There are many ranking 'providers' (see the Reference Section), and each will use different criteria. They can be helpful in the initial stages of selection. Look closely at what is actually being measured and how, before placing too much value on their determinations. All ranking systems provide a very limited picture of what is on offer: Beware of allowing them to limit your choice of university.

Lifestyle Considerations

In addition to cost, there are many other factors you need to think about, including location, size, social life, and student services.

The United States is geographically diverse. Before choosing a university, it is important for you to consider what type of climate suits you best. You may have enjoyed your Easter break in Florida, but are you prepared for the summer heat or lack of a winter? Or you may think you like snow, but are you prepared to have to shovel your way across campus in -40 degrees while studying in Buffalo? Do you prefer an urban or rural setting? While it may be exciting to think of yourself in a great city, the costs of living there are often much higher – will your budget stretch? Also, bear in mind that students in large cities may feel more socially isolated than those who choose a rural school. Conversely, a college that is miles away from any city may have more campus-based activities, but you may find not being able to escape to a nearby city induces claustrophobia and that relying upon the university for socializing is too restrictive.

If you attend a very small college, will seeing the same 500 people very week be too insular for you? Will you feel like a number if you re one of 60,000 at a large public university?

There are no right or wrong answers. Investigate each university and be honest about what type of environment you will be comfortable in. Take a critical look at the university's office for international students, and at the number of such students in attendance. While many enjoy being the lone 'foreigner' and having to fend for themselves, others find comfort in having a well-run place to go when homesick or confused and others with whom to share the same dilemmas.

Our Guide to Universities

In the next section of this book we examine in detail some of the many excellent colleges America has to offer. In choosing which schools to write about, we have considered a wide range of criteria. We look at vast state universities and small liberal arts colleges. We examine institutions on the East Coast, on the West Coast and those scattered in between. We look at places that produce artists and places that produce nuclear scientists. We look at the oldest of American colleges and at ones that are only just beginning to make a splash. We are unable to look at them all, but we hope we have provided an insight into most of the different types available.

There are certain qualities that the institutions we have chosen have in common. We have tried to cover universities that combine good academic reputations with sizeable international populations. Many of them offer financial aid, in one form or another, to international applicants. And all of them are looked upon favourably by those in the know. We hope the following guide is helpful to you, not as a comprehensive list of the places you should consider, but as an insight into the workings of some of the colleges that may well draw your attention.

Amherst College

Amherst, Massachusetts
www.amherst.edu
1,800 undergraduates

How many students does it take to change a light bulb at Amherst? Thirteen – one to change the bulb and an a cappella group to immortalize the event in song.

Take every stereotype you can imagine about New England colleges: the Puritan ethic, the white wooden buildings, the preppy students, the snow ... compile them all and you will have a fairly accurate vision of Amherst. This small college has long been hailed as one of the best of its kind in America, consistently coming at the top of the liberal arts rankings. Small in size and intimate in feel, it offers those addicted to the boarding-school experience new avenues of enjoyment and independence with all those old, secure home comforts.

The Campus

Amherst proudly labels itself the 'Fairest College' and it certainly has the charming New England feel that many Brits envision when they imagine an American university. The campus extends over 1,000 acres and is located on a hill. Old brick buildings jostle with newer and less successful architectural attempts, but the whole is successful and easy to find your way around.

The Amherst student body congregates around a few main buildings. The sporty head for the new and extensive Wolff Fitness Center while the Keefe Campus Center offers dramatic and social service groups a place to go. And everyone meets in the dining hall for meals. Students live in former fraternity houses or new buildings and living groups can range from the peace-loving loner to the party-favouring ten-man suites. However, wherever you end up, the small size of the student body makes it impossible to leave a room without running into someone you know. All freshmen are assigned housing and the bonds forged in this initial year often define the rest of your college living experience.

The People

Preppy is not really a word that has an equivalent in the English educational system. Our nearest counterpart is a combination of rugger buggers, Sloane rangers and Tim-nice-but-dim. Yet even this does not come close to the good old WASPs of New England. Amherst has never quite escaped its reputation as being one of the most preppy of the small American colleges, and a large percentage of its undergrad body have been turned out of the country club attending, Abercrombie and Fitch wearing, jeep driving mould.

This is not to say that Amherst is totally without diversity. In fact it prides itself on its open admission policies and estimates that around 30% of its undergraduate body are minority students. For the average British student, given the somewhat heterogeneous nature of most of our schools, it will probably seem a hot bed of diversity. And while its international intake is not as large as at some other schools, it is still substantial. After all, where Prince Albert of Monaco goes, others are sure to follow ...

One of the great advantages of the Amherst experience comes from the small size of its undergraduate class. With only around 400 students in each year, it is difficult for social divisions or exclusive cliques to survive. Everyone knows everyone else. When such a limited number are eating, living and working together, it is not easy to remain just a face in a crowd. This small-town environment is great for those who feel comfortable having their every move known. Yet it can be difficult for people who prefer the social whirl and comfortable anonymity of being one among thousands. And once you're established, it becomes ever harder to reinvent yourself.

While it is difficult to generalize, Amherst types tend to be outdoorsy, social and sporty. It is estimated that around 80% of students take part in some form of sport, with 30% playing at varsity level. Despite its small size, Amherst enjoys a great sporting reputation. The annual football game with Williams is the small college equivalent of the Harvard–Yale game (or the Oxbridge boat race). Crew is also popular – in keeping with the school's clean-cut image. The fantastic sporting facilities make this a great place to attend if you are an ardent jock. Come winter, the mountains are near enough to make skiing a weekend possibility, and hikes and camping sessions are a regular part of many students' leisure pursuits.

Hitting the Books

Amherst devotees believe that no college can rival their own in the realm of liberal arts. They take pride in the fact that this is a college where complete freedom of choice is encouraged. Students have only one requirement – the interdisciplinary Freshman Seminar. After that, they are free to design their own curriculum, constrained only by the guidelines of their major or, in the case of many, a double major. This flexibility is great for those individuals who are scared off by the prospect of mandatory core curriculum classes in subjects that they joyfully abandoned post-GCSE. Students should bear in mind that one of the great things about a liberal arts environment such as Amherst is that it allows you room to experiment – something that most British universities regard with great disapproval. The majority of students at Amherst have a reputation for taking full advantage of this. And, despite its easygoing atmosphere, there are a high proportion of ambitious honours students.

This means that those students who aim to get through their university career without ever interacting with a professor should not even contemplate Amherst. This is a college that prides itself on student–faculty relationships, and the small size of the campus makes this intimacy almost impossible to avoid. With an average class size of just nineteen, parents will certainly feel that their precious children are getting the attention they deserve. The children, meanwhile, may wish that they were getting a little less. Professors expect you to talk to them about your aims, problems and queries, and they are always available. In fact it is difficult not to run into them on a daily basis. If you are the type of person who needs a certain amount of care and intimacy with those around you (whether this involves knowing your professor's cat's name or hanging out with your dining hall server), Amherst is an ideal college.

This is not to say that Amherst undergraduates can expect a pampered existence. This is a challenging and highly competitive school and the renowned Puritan work ethic is an integral part of campus life. The faint-hearted or easily embarrassed should beware. Professors expect a great deal of verbal interaction from their students, and the intimate class sizes mean that a reluctance to participate is swiftly noticed. The idea of a 'mutual education' is much touted at Amherst. The general idea is that everyone learns from each other, bringing together the future hopes of America in informative and improving debate. While this may be an academic's pipe-dream, this is certainly not a campus where you should expect your views to go unheard or unchallenged.

Considering the smaller size of its faculty and the absence of a grad school, Amherst offers a large number of classes in a wide variety of subjects. However, if you have already read the course catalogue a thousand times and still find nothing that interests you, you have the great option of being able to take courses at four other universities. Amherst is part of the Five Colleges Coalition – which includes Smith, Mount Holyoke, Hampshire College and UMass Amherst (don't get confused). Cross-college enrolment is encouraged and very easy to do, allowing you to pick the best of not just one college but five.

Outside Those Ivory Walls

Upon arrival at Amherst, many find it difficult to discern where the college stops and the town begins. The town of Amherst is dominated by its colleges. With five major schools so close, it is a bustling student centre – a relief for those who find the Amherst campus and its students a little too limiting. Amherst is also a perfect example of a Massachusetts town, pretty, puritanical and with strong literary and historical roots. It was here that the famous American poetess, Emily Dickinson, locked herself up in her room for many years, churning out her poems (a situation to which many come to relate in their senior year).

Although Amherst is a relatively small town, its large student population means that most of your needs will be met. Cafés, restaurants and coffee shops abound, although by the end of four years you may feel that you have exhausted all social options. Amherst is situated about two hours' drive from Boston and three hours' drive from New York City. But while people talk about taking weekend road-trips to these two cities, it rarely happens, especially once the long, cold, New England winter sets in. Amherst students tend to be of the type happiest to stick in one place and not needing the bustle of a big city to entertain themselves on a Saturday night. If you prefer clubs to charm and sun to snow, then this may not be the place for you.

Social Life

The school may be small, the work may be hard, but the party spirit lives on – Amherst's social life closely resembles that of some English colleges. Rather than the Oxford bop, Amherst students enjoy the weekly TAP (which imaginatively stands for The Amherst Party). These school-wide events feature different themes, music and the ubiquitous keg. Despite its Massachusetts locale, Amherst does not subscribe to prohibition ideas, and Brits will be relieved to find that alcohol, most specifically beer, is a key part of student life. If you are teetotal there are many other social options – ranging from coffee shops to campus movies to the numerous clubs and societies.

Dating is not, however, a part of the Amherst students' life. The small size of the campus means that your random 'hook-ups' swiftly come back to haunt you. Thus, most people are either in near-marriage relationships or constantly on the look-out for fresh blood. Luckily the nearby colleges – most specifically the crowds at UMass – offer much needed social alternatives.

Getting In

Amherst may not be one of the Ivy League, but its admissions process is as competitive as any that you are likely to meet in America. This is partly due to its size.

Over 5,000 apply each year for around 400 places, and only 18% are admitted. A strong application is thus vital. Amherst is like other colleges in requiring the SAT Reasoning and three SAT IIs. A particular emphasis is placed on writing. This is a place where almost all subjects require a constant churning out of words, and your application form is a good place to show your mastery of the English language! An SAT II in writing is also looked upon favourably, although not required.

Good scores aside, you will need to demonstrate another dazzling side to your character to stand a chance. The Amherst admissions officers are very particular in selecting students whom they think will suit the school. It is thus important to convey in your application why you know that Amherst is the place for you. There is no particular Amherst type, but a life outside academia and an ability to fit into a community are prerequisites. Bear in mind that Amherst does not offer any interviews so the application form is your one opportunity to show them what you are made of.

There is an Early Decision option available to Amherst, but you must be absolutely sure that this is the one place you want to go. Once you hear back from them, the decision is binding. Amherst, however, never takes more than 30% of each class from the early application pool, so it is probably a good idea to give yourself more options and apply regularly. If you have your heart set on a gap year, be reassured. Amherst is one of the few colleges actively to encourage this.

Amherst offers no financial aid to international students. There may be a couple of scholarships available each year, but most Brits find it an expensive option.

Famous Grads
Clarence Birdseye – of Birdseye peas fame
Calvin Coolidge – US President
Albert Grimaldi – Prince of Monaco

Brown

Providence, Rhode Island
www.brown.edu
5,500 undergraduates, 1,500 graduates

How many students does it take to change a light bulb at Brown? Eleven – one to change the light bulb and ten to share the experience.

Do you have a hint of Eurotrash in your character? Or do you prefer hugging trees and making your own clothes? Whether you tend towards the jet set or the hippy, Brown University provides a liberal and all-encompassing campus environment with a prestigious academic reputation. In recent years this combination has attracted an increasing number of Brits to a school that is widely regarded as one of the best, and most fun, on the East Coast.

The Campus

Brown follows the New England trend – a beautiful campus, old brick buildings, the occasional bell tower. Founded in its present location in 1770, the campus is centred around the College Green. It is a charming, almost picture-perfect place – the type that producers of the typical East Coast college movie dream about. As a result, most students will find themselves living in pretty housing. Some privileged first-years are even situated on 'the Green' in accommodation that rivals that of the most beautiful Oxbridge colleges. Of course Brown also has its share of notoriously monstrous pieces of architecture where an unfortunate few of you may end up living. The prime example is the concrete, moated Grad Center, designed to contain any student riots (Brown is a politically active place) and definitely the most confusing building on campus.

Brown is situated at the top of the steep College Hill, quite a climb from the town of Providence below. Fortunately for the chronically unfit or lazy, regular and cheap trolley buses connect the two. The views down over the city are great, but the location means that freezing winds make even the most hardened students wince. In fact, Brown, along with its sister New England colleges, is NOT the place to come if you are a sun lover. For 70% (at least) of the time you spend in school, there will be snow, ice, rain and wind of a kind that Great Britain is never unlucky enough to see.

The Brunonian

When Brown opened its doors to students in 1764, it was the only one of the then seven colleges in the United States to embrace individuals of all religious persuasions. More recently it was the first American college to elect an African-American woman as its President. Diversity and liberalism are the cornerstones of the Brown mentality. As a result there is really no such thing as the average Brown student. Unlike the homogeneous, Abercrombie and Fitch clad crowds that throng such campuses as Princeton, Brown genuinely succeeds in attracting students from a multitude of backgrounds.

This is particularly true as regards ethnic and geographical diversity. Brown's campus resembles nothing so much as a huge Benetton ad – with students of all colours, styles and characters. The admissions office makes a special effort to bring in students from across the States and further afield. Almost 30% of each class are minority students, and 10% of the student body is international. As a British student you can thus rest assured that you will not be regarded as a creature from outer space but as an essential part of the diversity in which Brown glories.

Once you enter the hallowed gates, the average Brown man (or woman) enjoys the reputation of being extremely tolerant. There are so many different types of people on campus that the eccentric habits and quirks of each are generally accepted by all the others. The Brown system of placing freshmen in units of 40–60 people and always with a roommate quickly accelerates the process of meeting a wide variety of people. Even if individuals do tend to segregate into cliques in their sophomore year, their initial exposure to a diverse group stands them in good stead.

That is not to say that there is not a degree of segregation at Brown. Perhaps because of the fact that there are so many different types of student, it is always easy for individuals to find like-minded peers. These social groups can become rather insular, and some Brown students complain of being solely associated with groups just because they happen to be aspiring thespians or of Asian extraction. The presence of fraternity (Greek) houses on campus also leads to a certain amount of self-segregation within the student body. Yet such self-segregating is more of a human trait than a Brunonian one, and the Brown administration does take steps to prevent it. One example of this battle for equality is that all fraternity parties held at Brown must be open to every student on campus. No door is ever shut in the face of a Brunonian unless he chooses to close it himself.

Brown is known for being one of the most politically active of the East Coast colleges. Students who apply there tend to be pretty passionate about their beliefs, and as a result there is a certain amount of vocalization. If you are a die-hard conservative who believes that George Bush is the best thing since sliced bread, then Brown may not be the perfect place for you – unless of course you relish political debate. For the most part, however, political beliefs of all kinds tend to be tolerated, and, unless you are looking for a fight, everyone seems to rub along together. Major national and international issues – such as American action in Iraq – may draw out large groups of protesters, but for the most part it is only the hardened activists who stand out on a daily basis.

Brown students do tend, like all Americans, to get involved in a large number of extra-curricular activities. Perhaps owing to the Brunonian's liberal slant, many of these involve social service of one kind or another. There are also great campus publications, a strong dramatic and musical presence, a well-regarded radio station and, of course, numerous political and social action groups. There is also a large amount of varsity sports available on campus.

While the opportunities available at Brown are plenty, many students moan about the lack of resources. Brown is a relatively poor university – nowhere near the English equivalent of poor – but still lacking the endowment of its Ivy League peers. As a result, some of the facilities have suffered. There is no concert hall and the sports facilities are badly situated and somewhat run down. The food also enjoys the reputation of being completely disgusting – although for those of us whose taste buds were annihilated long ago by British school dinners this should not be such a problem. This shortage of cash also affects the size of the financial aid package available to its applicants.

Despite this, however, Brown has become an increasingly popular destination for pond-hopping Brits over the past few years. Self-proclaimed 'Eurotrash' have hit the Brown campus in a way that few other schools have achieved. This is perhaps encouraged by its reputation as one of the most fun of the prestigious Ivy League schools. Whatever the reason, the Brown campus is crowded with wealthy Europeans and Americans, sailing types who want to take advantage of Newport and party types who want to take advantage of the fun night life.

Hitting the Books

Choice. Freedom. Choice. This would surely be a better motto for the Brown shield than the somewhat clichéd '*In Deo Speramus*'. Brown stands out from other universities in the flexibility, or indeed absence, of its academic requirements. Students are expected to choose their own path, not plod along the one laid out for them some hundred years before. The official line is that each individual is the 'architect' of his or her educational experience. If you are the kind of person in possession of a great deal of personal motivation and initiative, then the Brown system can make you the architect of great things. If, however, you need strong academic guidance and supervision, then your own piece of Brunonian architecture could turn out more hut-like than palatial.

Brown has no core requirements. For some British students this can be a great thing. If, after your GCSEs, you swore that never again would you look at a chemical equation or critique a sonnet, this flexibility seems the ideal situation. The courses are there if you want to take them, but you are never compelled into doing something from which you automatically recoil. Yet this can also be a bad thing. One of the facets of the American educational system that draws Brits across the pond is the fact that it insists on maintaining the breadth of its liberal arts reputation. Unlike the unbending focus of the English universities, American colleges believe that a broad base of knowledge is important to one's education. And, even if you protest, the majority of American schools, with their core requirements, insist on it anyway. The fact that Brown allows you to circumnavigate this part of the liberal arts education is great for those who would prefer to embrace it in their own way. Yet for those who will not, it can erase an important part of the American educational experience.

Brown's sole requirements are that a student passes thirty classes and takes at least eight that qualify them for a major. Each major has different requirements, so some students will end up taking the vast majority of their courses in a specific area. The lack of initial core requirements allows students to experiment within the different departments before deciding on the direction they wish to pursue. Throughout their college experience they are provided with advisors who help them to formulate plans and make decisions.

Brown students definitely have a lot of personal contact with their professors – the student-faculty ratio is 8:1. Although Brown does have a graduate school, it is the undergrad body that attracts the most focus – a far cry from some of the bigger research institutions in the United States. Relationships between professor and student are notably relaxed – often on a first name basis. This interaction is something that many English universities simply do not offer. Brown prides itself on its small class sizes (around 30), and in such an environment there is a chance to develop a real relationship with those instructing you. As has been mentioned, Brown is a place that believes in self-vocalization, and class discussion and participation is normally an important part of one's grade.

And speaking of grades ... one of the unique and, to many, very attractive things about the Brown academic system is the ability to take any class that you want on a pass/fail (or S/NC – Satis-factory/No Credit) basis. The idea behind this is that it gives the students a chance to experiment. Those history of art majors with a sudden interest in biochem can take the course without fearing their letter grade. Some abuse this system – taking classes without doing any of the work – but for the most part it is another good example of the way in which Brown gives its students as much flexibility as possible.

Brown has not escaped the taint of grade inflation that has dragged such schools as Harvard into recent media attacks. Grades on campus seldom fall below a B and are often higher. Anything below a C is a fail – although students can withdraw from classes at the very last moment and it would be a real achievement to actually fail out. The university also never releases these grades to the ouside world – another means of encouraging students to experiment and of reducing academic pressure.

Brown students are often laughed at by their Ivy League peers for being slackers who never have to fulfil any real requirements. Yet the academic standard, resources and professor accessibility at Brown are as high as at any of its contemporaries. It is the flexibility of the system that leads to this reputation. Those who need a more rigorous academic structure should probably avoid Brown, but, for those who like to follow their own paths while always having support behind them, the Brown experience is a great one to choose.

Social Life

Brown is known for being a fun place. It caters for all social preferences, whether they involve hard-core socializing or an evening spent in a coffee house with two friends. The campus itself has a number of fraternities – both of the traditional Greek variety, and individual co-ed, Jewish or literary equivalents. Around 10% of the men on campus are involved with one of these, and 2% of the women. The parties they throw every weekend are always open to all, but most students prefer to forge their own social lives. There is always something to do at night at Brown – although many students favour smaller gatherings to the keg stands and noise of these larger parties.

The campus itself offers the entertainments of the busy Thayer Street – a social centre for Brown students looking for companionship and caffeine. If this becomes too boring, then there is always the alternative venue of Providence – a city that offers students good restaurants, jazz and fun clubs. Off-campus parties are also extremely popular – fewer people and less rules, making them more attractive to many than those parties held at Brown itself. Europeans tend to dominate certain parts of the Brown social scene, and clubs such as Viva become an East Coast substitute for the lures of Chinawhite's – attracting the Eurotrash set (many of whom are British and Greek).

No Brit should expect their American social experience to be akin to their friends drinking their way through the British universities. Even at Brown, a place known for its fun environment, ID checking can be strict – one of the least fun parts of New England life. (Foreign students however are lucky, passports are not normally ID'd). There is also no real long-term dating scene. You may see many of your friends back home in near-marriage type situations, but Brown students state that those in long-term relationships are in the minority on campus.

Outside Those Ivory Walls

Providence, Rhode Island, is a place on the up. Recently voted the least polluted and safest city in the nation, it provides a welcome social alternative for Brown students. Many, in fact, choose to stay there after graduation – true testimony to the charms of the place. Recently there has been a large effort to rebuild downtown Providence – an action that has increased its appeal as one of the most attractive New England cities. While it lacks the size and national clout of New York and Boston, Providence is known for having great restaurants (probably owing to its large Italian population), fun clubs and a strong musical reputation. Jazz, pop singers and student bands all enjoy large and enthusiastic audiences.

Brown students love Providence because it provides them with a metropolitan alternative to campus life while avoiding the hectic pace of bigger cities. Brown's location just above the town also gives students the chance to have an urban college experience without losing the campus feel. The presence of the prestigious art school RISD (Rhode Island School of Design) just down the hill from Brown also adds to the fun, student atmosphere of the city, and there is a fair amount of communication between the two schools. Should you feel the need to escape, there are easy bus and train services to both Boston (one hour) and New York (four hours).

Getting In

It's tough. Brown is a highly competitive college to gain admittance to. Approximately 15,000 students apply each year, of which only 2,500 are accepted. The admissions process is a challenging one. Not only are high academic standards expected (most students score at least 1400 on the SAT I), but the admissions office also seeks out those students with diverse interests or qualities that stand out from the crowd.

Applicants are expected to take SAT I and three SAT IIs. There is also the opportunity (recommended but not required) to have an interview with Brown alumni. They will get in contact with you, and there are normally a fair amount of them scattered around the UK. These interviews also give you an opportunity to ask about Brown. Brown is also one of the only colleges to ask you to submit a photo – cynics state that this is why the campus is continually voted most attractive. So get prepared to look your best!

Perhaps the most important part of the admissions process at Brown is the personal essay that all applicants must write. Every school claims that it is looking beyond academics to the individual, and this is certainly true to an extent. At Brown, however, it really is an essential part of the admissions process and gives you a great chance to promote your own thoughts, ideas and personality. The fact that they require you to handwrite it is testament to quite how much it provides them with a chance to analyse your character! When filling out the endless forms and writing the essay, it is important to bear in mind that admissions officials want to see things that distinguish you from the crowd of other eager applicants.

As with most universities, Brown has both an Early Action option and a Regular Decision plan. Its website offers more information on current deadlines for these. There is a limited, and definitely not plentiful, amount of financial aid available for international students. It MUST be applied for at the time of admission – all later applications are simply dismissed.

Famous Grads

John D. Rockefeller, Jr – philanthropist extraordinaire
JFK, Jr – journalist – just as cool as his father, and as tragic
Kenneth Starr – you too could prosecute Bill Clinton

California, oh California

It is easy for the Brits to forget quite how huge America really is. Viewing it from our warped Atlantic perspective, we tend to focus in on a few key cities and forget about the vast expanse of land that divides them. It is easy to believe that New York, Chicago and Los Angeles are adjacent stops along an M4 equivalent – easily accessible from one another and culturally similar. That is, until we are reminded that there is a ranch in Texas, inhabited solely by a few hundred head of cattle, which is the same size as England. America prides itself upon its diversity, its wealth of cultural variety and the vast discrepancies that its nation manages to encompass. It is impossible to generalize about a nation with so many contradictions. Just as the *Economist* once got into trouble for writing, 'It was raining in America', so will you find that stating you are interested in 'university in America' will fall far short of satisfactory.

While you may pride yourself upon an adventurous spirit in choosing to attend a university 3,000 miles away, you should never forget that many of those Americans who share your rooms and classes have travelled an equally long distance. And, if you think that informing your parents that you are going to be in New York for the next four years is difficult, you should try telling them that LA is your destination of choice. Yet, while doubling the distance from home may be hard, there are many massive benefits. Traditionally, the elite (for which read snobbish) East Coast institutions have dismissed their younger Californian peers as nouveau and overly liberal. (Such insults may well be recompense for those suffered by the Harvards and Princetons at the hands of the Oxbridge bastion.) The Californians have not been deterred, however, and the Stanfords, UCLAs and CalTechs of the West Coast have proved themselves as leaders on a worldwide academic footing. Students from all over the States have been quick to embrace the idea of spending four years in constant sunshine, in easy reach of the beach, mountains, ski slopes and the odd desert (not to mention the lights of Hollywood). The chance of combining an OC life with a degree from one of the several Californian institutions, consistently ranked among the best in the world, is one that you would have to be foolish not to take into consideration.

There are a plethora of good Californian schools available, and not all of them can be covered in this guide. A university tour to the West Coast is highly recommended, but, for those of you unable to muster up the air miles, here is a quick guide to some of the best Californian campuses.

The UC Schools

The state educational system in American can be rather hit and miss, but Californian students are secure in the knowledge that their state offers some of the best public higher education around. Both UC Berkeley and UCLA are covered extensively in this guide, but prospective students should also consider UC San Diego (known for its strong science programmes), UC Santa Cruz (great for relaxation and beautiful people) and UCSB (a relaxed, beachside education with a strong academic reputation).

CalTech

Often referred to as the MIT of the West Coast, this tiny institution boasts the same number of nerds but in sunshine. CalTech's reputation in science and technology is almost unparalleled, and it continues to attract the very best of the best. Set in Pasadena, California, this hugely popular college is known for its world-class facilities and eclectic group of students. No one at CalTech does anything by halves – the workload is incredibly intense, the IQ average incredibly high and the campus incredibly beautiful. And it has produced even more Nobel Prize winners than MIT! If you are the next nuclear physicist or if you simply like a combination of frat houses and building space rockets, then this is a great place to consider. But start working now, this is a VERY competitive institution and there are only around 200 spots in each class.

Pomona

This popular university is known for its extremely involved faculty and its relaxed social scene. Good for students who want a sound education in an environment that will guide them every step of the way. Pomona is a fairly small college but offers a wide variety of academic choices. While it is not situated in any of the great Californian cities, Pomona makes up for its lack of external options with a lively on-campus party scene. Even at the end of four years, most students don't want to leave.

USC

Long known as the 'University of Spoilt Children', the University of Southern California has established itself as a college that spoils its students rotten. Occupying an ideal location (10 minutes from the beach, right next to Hollywood), USC has also managed to bring together an extremely diverse student body in an excellent academic environment. USC students really do have it all – an excellent and relaxed faculty, a well-integrated community and a beautiful campus. This could be the closest you get to OC living – so don your cutest clothes and start working on that tan!

Stanford

Internationally known for its students, its athletes and its vision, Stanford is covered in depth on p. 153.

UCLA

Los Angeles, California
www.ucla.edu
25,300 undergraduates, 12,166 graduates

How many students does it take to change a light bulb at UCLA?
Five – one to change the light bulb and four to find the perfect J.
Crew outfit to wear for the occasion.

For those Brits who have always longed for the bright lights and laid-back lifestyle of the West Coast, UCLA is an option that should definitely be taken into consideration. The fortunes of UCLA and the surrounding city of Los Angeles have always been linked. Over the past century, both have grown beyond their founders' wildest dreams and both now enjoy prosperity and a certain superstar status. Certainly, UCLA is one of America's top universities; a veritable metropolis, it boasts superb facilities, beautiful weather, top academic ratings and varsity teams that regularly fill up Olympic spots. As part of the California state system, however, around 90% of places are filled by Californian students. Aside from heightening the competition for international students, this requirement also means that any Brits applying must be able to embrace the Californian lifestyle. Still, with the Pacific Ocean just five minutes away, star-studded Beverley Hills just down the road and access to some of the brightest (and most laid-back) of America's academics, many would agree that the cultural adjustment required is not that much of a burden!

The Campus
UCLA is HUGE! With just under 40,000 full-time students and the faculty and other staff to match, it is closer to a city than a normal campus school. Indeed it even has its own hospital on site. Founded

in the 1880s, it moved to its present location in 1929 and since then has grown (like the city that surrounds it) at an exponential rate. The four original buildings survive and the campus, while lacking the quaintness of the New England schools, has an architectural charm of its own. The beautiful weather, palm trees and proximity of both mountains and ocean undoubtedly help, but the dormitories and classrooms are an aesthetic success in their own right. From the great Powell library to the more modern quarters (all in the middle of being corrected for any seismic calamities), the buildings serve to unite the vast campus into a pleasing whole and give students a break from the pulsating city that surrounds them. Be warned, however – despite its overall attractiveness, the grounds are not easy to get around and not all the accommodation on offer may reach the expectations of your California dreaming.

While UCLA consists of a number of different undergraduate and graduate schools, the majority of undergrads will find themselves as students at the College of Letters and Sciences. This academic institution has traditionally divided itself (both geographically and socially) into two halves. This split is made along the line of intellectual preference (or, as the Bruins would have it, each individual is categorized by their level of geekiness). The North Campus is the home of the humanities – attracting those interested in the liberal arts, media or social studies. This is also the spiritual home of the many 'beautiful people' (for which one can often read wealthy West Coast kids with daddy's credit card). Meanwhile, the South Campus calls out to the scientists, the engineers and those who choose to spend their days staring at test tubes, in other words the brains of the operation. While such sweeping generalizations are obviously mostly inaccurate, a certain amount of rivalry continues to exist between the halves, and various disparaging comments about brainpower and beauty are constantly fired across the boundary.

UCLA is fortunate enough to enjoy a great setting within the heart of a bustling city and a large amount of space for its students to play, work and live in. Given their prime location, and presumably the expense of nearby real estate (Beverley Hills is just down the road), most students choose to live in campus dormitories during their first year. The university offers a number of different housing options, including various themed floors – for those who want to bond with fellow artists or mountain climbers. These dorms form the basis of most students' friendship groups, and, while in later years it is common to move out into the university apartments situated on the southwest side of the campus, it is extremely sensible to stay on campus for your freshman year. After all, in a university with this many people, good bands of friends are important to come by.

The Bruin

How can one possibly define a UCLA student? Given the sheer numbers of them, it is safest to say that they defy generalization – except perhaps for a hearty love of their alma mater and a propensity for wearing the colours blue and gold. It is also a given that the vast majority will be Californians. Many myths about the West Coaster have reached English ears. They are all hippies, health freaks, obsessed with the environment, into technology, and bent on fame and fortune in entertainment. While some of these rumours are true (health is very big – it comes from being able to run outside in fetching bikinis while getting a tan), California encompasses a huge variety of individuals. From its ranches and its beaches, its mountains and its deserts, its cities and its hamlets, Californian teenagers set out en masse and head for UCLA. So, while your English accent is bound to make you stick out like a sore thumb, you should be aware that not everyone around you came from the same high school. And, you carry the trump card – as an alien from out-of-state, everyone is going to want to visit you!

The sunshine in California has a great effect on the population, and the majority of the students pride themselves on their laid-back attitude to life. Certainly, everyone on the West Coast seems friendly and happy. However, UCLA is a very competitive school and everyone is aware that a certain amount of work is necessary to maintain the right grades. Thus, although some sunbathing goes on, it is accompanied with a degree of hard work. Students often report that, owing to the curve on which UCLA grading operates, there can be a degree of rivalry over academic placings. So, if you get stuck on that biochem homework, don't expect your classmates to be bending over backwards to help you work it out.

Yet, while academics may raise the odd hackle, the Bruins tend to be more united than divided. UCLA is a university possessed by a huge amount of school spirit, and events such as Homecoming, the famous Beat SC Week and even Engineering Week (OK, so it's not all cool) attract huge numbers of people. UCLA is one of the top sporting teams of the nation – in fact its athletes have won an extraordinary 195 Olympic medals since 1920. Whether you are a fan of football, which reaches its climax with the huge annual match against USC, or of basketball, in which case you may well be camping out during March Madness, you are sure to find a stadium full of fellow hooligans with whom to celebrate or commiserate. And you can take pride in the fact that, unlike those sad excuses that pass for East Coast teams, your school is unrivalled throughout the US of A.

For the large proportion of UCLA students who are not preparing to be drafted into the NBA, there are many other options available. Despite the laid-back attitude that Californians pride themselves upon, almost every Bruin is involved with at least one extra-curricular activity. From writing for the *Daily Bruin*, which is one of the largest daily newspapers in LA, to community service in one of the less privileged parts of the city, there are literally hundreds of activities available. And while the lazy may shrink from these energetic pursuits, all of these extra-curricular options are instrumental in helping you form a social group, meet new people, cement old friendships and appreciate the amazing city in which you are spending four years of your life.

California is one of the most diverse states in the country and you should be prepared for a similar variety of ethnic, religious and financial backgrounds among your classmates. Although UCLA is known to have more than its fair share of rich Cali kids, they are diluted somewhat by many students from less privileged backgrounds. Colourwise, the number of whites is equalled by the number of Hispanics and Asians – nicely completing the Benetton ad effect. Yet, while ethnic diversity certainly exists in numbers, many students complain that social groups tend to divide themselves upon ethnic or financial lines. You, as the weird foreigner who defies all American categories, have the perfect excuse to plough into each and every group and establish friendships as you go. But make sure you do this from the beginning – in such a sea of faces it is easy to become just one of an extremely large crowd.

Hitting the Books

There can be no denying the fact that UCLA provides its students with a sound education. The majority of Americans will argue that you will receive a stronger academic experience among a more diverse group of people down the road at Stanford or even at the sister-school of UC Berkeley, but few will find too much to complain about at UCLA. The real problem lies in the fact that, on such a huge campus, a much larger effort is required if you are to make your mark – both academically and socially. While your accent will at least help your professors to distinguish you from all of those Californians, the transition from even the largest of secondary schools will be immense. The old granny maxim of 'from a big fish in a small pond to a little lost tadpole' seems very appropriate.

This sense of isolation is not helped by the fact that classes at UCLA are, by necessity, rather larger than those at smaller schools. This means that, even if you are being taught by the leader of his or her academic field (and UCLA has many of these), you may still be unable to spend any time interacting with them on a personal basis. Many at UCLA complain that professors, while fascinating individuals and renowned researchers, are not very good at actually communicating with the lowly students who sit before them three times a week. Bridging this gap is important if you are to make the most of your academic experience at UCLA, but you may have to fight your way through the crowds of other overachievers bent on the same mission.

This is not to say that the academic system at UCLA does not have its advantages. For one thing, the university has some of the best resources around, and the library and research opportunities are wonderful. UCLA is also one of the few universities that chooses not to follow the semester system. Instead it works on a three-quarter system. Many enjoy this as it means that they get to experience more classes during their time at university. This is particularly beneficial if you find that you seriously misjudged quite how interesting Geology 101 was going to be. However, it also means that you have less time per class and face exams on a more regular basis. For those who fear that continual assessment will be one of the more stressful parts of the American experience, UCLA could turn out to be a nightmare. But for those who are good at exams and want to have a chance to experience every possible course, it might be a dream come true.

For the first two years, most students will find they are taking lower-division courses. These consist of the broad and often introductory classes that help you to decide what direction you want to head in when you finally choose your major. This is done at the beginning of your third year (giving you lots of time to make up and then change your mind). After that you embark on upper-division classes that focus on specific departments and are smaller in size. Certain departments are particularly strong – the film programme is one of the most famous in the country. Whatever your major, students also face a type of core curriculum in the shape of a GE (or general education) class. These courses, also known as 'cluster courses', span a year and allow you to experience academic disciplines that range across a variety of departments – in effect operating as a whistle-stop tour of all the options that await your final academic decisions. Because they last for a year, they also provide you with an opportunity to cement both social and academic relationships at an early point in your student career.

Social Life
On your first day at UCLA you are more than likely to be overwhelmed. The thousands of people, all sporting cute Californian tans and laid-back attitudes, may send you into unexpected pangs of homesickness for the grey skies and grotty pubs of good old England. But by day two you will undoubtedly have discovered that, not only does everyone else feel just as lost as you, but there are so many people here and so many things to do that it is near impossible to be left out in the cold.

Your social life at UCLA is something you can really choose to mould for yourself. While smaller colleges, such as Williams or Carleton, mean that you have no choice but to befriend everyone in your class, UCLA offers an almost unlimited option of people. Much of the social scene here is influenced by which of the many groups with whom you identify yourself. People tend to peel off according to their interests – but it is perfectly possible to avoid being typecast. If you are an avid scientist who enjoys surfing, chances are you'll find people who feel the same way.

The actual patterns of the social scene may be a little more difficult for the average Brit to work out. For one thing, all that sunshine and beach living takes a certain amount of adjustment. Parties on the UCLA campus, and after a Bruin victory there are parties like you have never seen before, take place in a variety of guises. Whether you are heading for one of the glitzier LA bars, partying in one of the frats that around 10% of the campus choose to join or merely thrashing out a play-by-play in Starbucks, you will rarely be short of a place to go on a Saturday night.

Outside Those Ivory Walls

City of Angels, home to the stars, dwelling place of supermodels and surfers – Los Angeles will provide you with a university experience you could never get anywhere else. Whether you are rollerblading (and star-spotting) in Beverly Hills, studying marine biology on one of the beautiful Pacific beaches or catching up on some culture at the Getty Centre, you can be sure that you will accumulate more than enough stories to make your friends back home green with envy. Anyone who is bored while at UCLA must accept the fact that life itself will probably prove a disappointment. Whatever your taste – whether it be partying till dawn or retiring to bed after a fourteen-mile hike – you can be sure that it will be catered for here. And with an undergraduate body that beats many towns for size, you will also always be able to find people who are prepared to share the experience with you.

One of the reasons UCLA kids are always on the move is the diversity of the city they inhabit. California is one of those rare places that is able to offer beaches, mountains, cities and deserts, all in one fell swoop. Los Angeles may not be everyone's cup of tea – the aspiring actors and constant beauty and health regimes may drive some round the bend – but you would be hard pressed to dislike everything. For lovers of the great outdoors, there are hiking opportunities aplenty and skiing a couple of hours away in the winter. For those who march to a rather different beat, clubs of every variety and some of the best bars and restaurants in the world can be found just around the corner (providing your credit card can keep up!). And with a great public transport system, nothing is inaccessible.

Having said that, many UCLA students find that everything they need for a successful student life is right on their doorstep. Westwood Village (like no English village you have ever seen) has more than its fair share of student hangouts, offering a more affordable and often more friendly option to those who shun the real world. And, with most off-campus houses located in this area, this atmosphere tends to exist around the clock. Meanwhile, for those who really want to escape, UCLA is a superb launch pad for one of the must-do American experiences, the road trip. Ever fancied a gamble at Las Vegas or a trip down to Central America? Find (or kidnap) a friend with a car, grab your toothbrush and off you go.

Getting In

Getting into UCLA is no walk in the park. To start with, unless you are a bona fide Californian, your chances are already slimmed to being one of the 10% of the student body that come from out-of-state. Although it is a huge student body (and bear in mind this means you stand more chance of admittance here than at UC Berkeley), this still narrows your chances considerably. UCLA loves having international students (adding as they do to the diversity of the school), but it simply cannot take as many of them as its privately run contemporaries. This limitation also means there is no financial aid or even scholarships available for us poor Brits, although it is always worth enquiring.

To reduce your chances even further, UCLA is also one of the most popular schools in America, frequently boasting of more applications than any other university. As the atmosphere is so competitive, top grades are a necessity as well as an ability to show a commitment to academia and other extra-curricular interests. The SAT I is required, as are three SAT IIs. Unusually, the SAT IIs are specified – one in writing, one in mathematics and one in a subject of your choice. A strong personal essay and good teacher recommendations are vital if you are to stand a chance of admission – a Californian driver's licence would stand you in even better stead. One ray of hope – your chances of being admitted are, in fact, better than those of Americans who do not live in California.

Famous Grads

Francis Ford Coppola – Mr Godfather himself
James Dean – if only all the students looked like this
Michael Ovitz – hooray for the Disney connection!

UC Berkeley

Berkeley, California
www.berkeley.edu
23,200 undergraduates, 12,883 graduates

How many students does it take to change a light bulb at Berkeley? 2,001 – one to demand his right not to change the bulb and 2,000 to organize the strike in support of him.

UCLA may be the giant of the University of California schools but its sister school, Berkeley, situated in the Bay Area outside San Francisco, is the older sibling. As the first of the Californian universities, Berkeley has earned the right to call itself simply 'Cal', and, for the 22,000 undergraduates enrolled, there is no question that this precedence is academic as well as chronological. National rankings consistently place Berkeley ahead of UCLA, and it draws crowds of ferociously intelligent and even more outspoken students from across the Golden State and beyond. The lure of being a mere ten miles away from San Francisco and yet completely ensconced in one of the most dynamic campuses in America is hard to resist.

Berkeley has always been the American university most known for its liberal attitude and democratic principles. The spirit that led to mass protests and riots in the 1960s continues to thrive today, and students are proud of the outspoken nature of their classmates and professors. If you are a shy and retiring flower with no opinion on politics and a preference for a cliquey environment, then Berkeley is definitely not the place for you. If, however, you enjoy making friends across diverse groups, wrangling with your professors and mounting your own soapbox in Sproul Plaza (the centre of campus debate and always home to at least eight different protests), then Berkeley is right up your street. Students adore the fact that this is a school that is proud to encourage independent thought, and you can rest assured that, no matter what your English eccentricities, you will find yourself valued and included.

School spirit runs high at UC Berkeley – probably helped by the fact that their mascot, the Californian Golden Bear (nicknamed Oski) is one of the cutest around. But Berkeley students do not limit their excitement about their community to chants at the huge football games, or mass attendance at such quirky traditions as the Daffodil Festival. Instead, students tend to be massively involved in any number of outreach groups, social programmes and mass activities. It is virtually impossible to get through college at Berkeley without getting roped into one of these, and most students find them to be the most valuable part of their entire experience. Indeed, the movement of UC Berkeley students after graduation reflects their dedication to college and the community – 'Cal' sends more students to the Peace Corps than any other school, while a huge proportion of others go on to do PhDs.

Berkeley's democratic principles also overflow into the classroom and the admissions policies. Students are actually able to teach their own classes if they are unable to find a faculty member already offering one. These are known as DECal classes (or Democratic Education at Cal) and they fall completely under a student's jurisdiction. In other respects, however, there are many similarities between an education at Berkeley and one at UCLA. Both schools are enormous, and prospective students need to be prepared to make much more effort to find an academic (and social) footing. Professors, often brilliant, are not at all keen to hold your hand, and, while the resources are there, the onus is on you to discover and use them. Competition is also rife, despite the laid-back appearance every student aims for, and independent thought is crucial if you are to succeed.

Admission into Berkeley is even harder for a Brit than admission into UCLA. Both universities fall under the same California quotas, but, as Berkeley has the (marginally) smaller campus, your chance of acceptance is even lower. Berkeley does, however, place great importance on personal characteristics and estimates that, while 50% of its choice is necessarily affected by grades, the other 50% depends on the leadership skills and individual strengths of each class of applicants. The SAT I and three SAT IIs are required, but, unusually, Berkeley does not request teacher recommendations or offer interviews to prospective students. This means that a huge amount depends on the strength of your personal statement. This focus on individuals, their views and their objectives nicely sums up the attitude of Berkeley throughout a student's university career.

Columbia

New York, New York
www.columbia.edu
7,100 undergraduates, 5,900 graduates

How many students does it take to change a light bulb at Columbia? Seventy-six – one to change the light bulb, fifty to protest the light bulb's right not to change, and twenty-five to hold a counterprotest.

New York, New York. For those who crave the bright lights of the big city, there is no better place to go to university. And there is no better university than Columbia College, the urbanite darling of the Ivy League. Columbia not only offers you immediate access to every metropolitan resource you can imagine, it manages to combine this with a campus that makes you part of a college community. And, when you're not out exploring Soho or jogging in Central Park, you are busy struggling with the homework that makes this one of the top educations in America. Strong academics, great school spirit and one of the most exhilarating environments in the world, this is a school where Saturday nights will never be dull.

The Campus
Columbia was founded in 1754, making it the fifth oldest college in the US. It was initially named King's College, but, after the Yankees decided they were better off without the Brits, its name was changed to reflect the roots of America. When it began, New York was far from the bustling city it is today, and Columbia was situated in what would now pass for the countryside. This may be the reason for the spacious campus environment, an unusual quality in a college surrounded by the big city. Students who crave the American-college feel will not lack quads, old brick buildings and beautiful architec-

ture – Columbia has managed to embark on the new without getting rid of the old.

Brits should, however, be warned that, if they are searching for an old-world East Coast campus feel, Columbia may prove a disappointment. The university is a huge institution that encompasses fifteen different undergrad and grad schools on its extensive Morningside Heights campus. As a result it feels like a little oasis of student life amid the stresses and strains of an adult city. Most of the faces in your immediate environment will be young ones, and the area is shaped by the students who live in it. Columbia College is a small enough school to have a real sense of community, but its existence inside a vast university means there are always new people to meet. And, for those men who get sick of Columbia girls, the close affiliation with the all-female Barnard College offers whole new avenues of exploration!

Student enjoyment of life on the Columbia campus is testified to by the fact that 90% of students choose to live there for their entire college career. Columbia has great housing, and 60% of students are guaranteed a single room. This may seem strange by English standards, but in America it is not unheard of to live in doubles for most of your college career. Most freshmen at Columbia choose to live in either Carman Hall or John Jay – buildings that inevitably turn into social centres for that class. On-campus accommodation is definitely the way to go – after all, who wants to pay the extortionate housing prices of NYC?

The Columbian

It takes a certain type of person to thrive at Columbia. New Yorkers are known for being as tough as they come and life at New York's top university follows this trend. Many quiet country mice will be turned off by the overwhelming nature of the big city, the constant noise and the proximity of Harlem – one of the least affluent and most criminal areas of Manhattan. Nor is this a school where the administration is prepared to baby you along. Columbia students (like thousands of their contemporaries) moan about the amount of work they are expected to do, the number of courses they have to take and the fact that the faculty expects a constant and high level of commitment from them. Yet, when questioned, they fiercely defend their school.

It seems that those who survive that initial 'sink or swim' feeling grow to love and appreciate both Columbia and New York for the independence their 'tough-love' approach inspires.

Although Columbia produces a class of highly independent and determined individuals with degrees in street smarts as well as academics, it does offer them a certain amount of help along the way. Columbia is well-known for the superiority of its advising system. This extends from the faculty to the in-dorm assistants, ensuring that you always have a place to go to with any questions. Columbia also has a nationally famous website 'Ask Alice' which answers any questions about sex, drugs, alcohol and general student debauchery that you could possibly think of posing.

Columbia students like to work hard but they also like to play hard. Luckily, this is a university that offers them the opportunity to do both. Columbia has great resources, great teaching and about a million and one extra-curricular pursuits that you can be involved in. Whether you are playing in orchestras, ripping up the sports pitches or taking part in the huge social action programmes that work with New Yorkers, chances are your schedule will fill up within days of arriving on campus. The Columbia atmosphere is not for the laid-back. The bustle of the busiest city in the world is right outside your doorstep and even the laziest students are energized by it. Furthermore, Columbia actively expects you to do more in life than academics (something that some of the more uptight East Coast universities could learn from). It is thus perfectly possible to take five classes, belong to two clubs and one sports team and still enjoy an active social life. Be warned though – your eight hours' sleep a night might suffer slightly!

One of the nicest things about Columbia is the amount of school spirit its students have. While students at colleges that bask at the top of the Ivy Leagues routinely bitch about their academic institutions, students at Columbia, a school that is normally ranked slightly lower, rave about their university. School events such as Homecoming (another of those bizarre American occasions involving sports teams and beer) help to increase this sense of belonging to the community. After all, how difficult is it to sport what has to be one of the nicest university colours (a perfect baby blue) and gather around one of the coolest university football symbols (the lion)?

Columbia students even managed to remain enthusiastic when their football team hit the infamous 'streak' of failure – forty-five games in a row! And in a sense this sums up the Columbian student – enthusiastic, optimistic and determined to succeed in a high-pressure and demanding environment.

Hitting the Books

Columbia College enjoys the unique position of maintaining an intimate academic community within a major and wealthy university. As such, its undergraduates have access to all the resources they could possibly want – including strings of research labs and an impressive college library. Yet, at the same time, they work in small classroom settings – around 70% of the classes have under twenty students – and thus benefit from actually having the attention of the professor. Sometimes this attention may seem a little much, especially for those British students who prefer to hide at the back of a large lecture hall. With a student–faculty ratio of 7:1, there is little escape – a disadvantage for those students hoping to breeze their way through college but, ultimately, one of Columbia's biggest strengths.

For while NYC offers Columbia students the chance to play hard, the faculty also expect them to work hard. This is a competitive environment and requires a certain amount of dedication. For one thing, Columbia students take five classes a semester, one more than the average number, and a significant juggling feat for those Brits who are used to specializing. But while the moans may go up around campus, this curriculum actually allows Columbian students a huge degree of flexibility in choosing their courses. The most popular majors include English, History and Politics, but many students choose to double major. The ultratalented, and ultraefficient, may even find time to do joint degrees with either the fantastic Juilliard school of music or the school of engineering.

Some Columbian students complain about the bureaucracy of their academic system and state that individual students have to be both assertive and energetic in finding out what they want to do. Columbia does not baby its students but, clichéd as it sounds, the more you put in, the more you get out. And, of course, you get to do it all in a centre that could not be more conducive to academic learning. Whether you're taking a history course, studying Egyptian art or struggling with the finer points of physics, New York is guaranteed to have a library, organization or exhibition just for you.

Core curricula are the dread of many British students heading across the Atlantic. After all, who wants to take more maths after finishing GCSEs? Columbia, however, is renowned for core classes which pride themselves on stimulating their students in intellectual discussion about the matters that are truly important to the world. This may all seem a bit pretentious, but students rave about the small seminars and the chance they get to pick apart the world's great philosophers, writers, artists and politicians on a weekly basis. This core curriculum spreads over the first two years and consists of an initial course in Literature Humanities (affectionately known as Lit. Hum.) and a sophomore course in Contemporary Civilization (CC). These courses are backed up with foreign language, science, music and writing classes. One of the great things about an American education is that it takes you in knowing nothing and spits you out knowing at least a little bit of everything. Columbia is the master at this, and many would argue there is no better or more comprehensive core education available. And, to top it all, you even get to do a year of mandatory PE – just when you thought you had left aerobics behind you for good!

Social Life

Columbia College offers a diverse community within a diverse city. Thus, whether your ideal Saturday night is spent at off-beat poetry readings fuelled by small black espressos, or at the most fashionable nightclubs fuelled by something even stronger, you are sure to find both the people and the place. New York City offers Columbian students a plethora of opportunities and, more importantly, the chance to kick off the campus dust from their heels and explore the wider world whenever they choose. And when they prefer to stay at home, Morningside Heights offers the typical student run of coffee shops, pizza parlours and cheap bars. These provide those crucial meeting points for the weekday nights when you are just dying to escape your dorm room. Luckily, the close community in the Columbia dorms means you are guaranteed other people to procrastinate with.

Columbia does have a Greek scene – not as strong as that of the

Southern schools – but still an important part of the university experience. This is welcome in so much as it provides you with a social forum that is open only to undergraduate students – giving you a chance to bond with your classmates as well as with the rest of the big bad city. There are twenty-two Greek organizations at Columbia, and the College estimates that between 10–15% of its students are affiliated with them. Aside from the parties, keg stands and eternal brother/sisterhood, these frats and sororities often offer an alternative place to base your social life. Many of them own pretty NY brownstone houses in the immediate area – allowing you to stumble out of the party and be home in five minutes.

Outside Those Ivory Walls

There is no better selling point for Columbia than New York City. This pseudo-capital of America is truly a town that never sleeps, and Columbia students have it all on their doorstep. Whether you want to go to an art gallery, cheer on the Yankees or hit the newest club, it's all just a cab ride away. And, while living in New York is expensive, Columbia students quickly learn the best ways to negotiate the city. Anxious parents might worry about the dangers of sending their kiddies off to the big bad city. Certainly, New York has its fair share of crimes, but, owing to the lock-em-up attitude of Giuliani, the city has become a much safer place. Columbia dorms all have great security, and, provided you use your common sense, New York is as safe as anywhere else.

And, for those stay-at-homes who can't be bothered to walk to the subway station, Morningside Heights offers a great campus environment. In recent years it has been filled with student hangouts – from diners to coffee houses and laundromats. Now Columbia students do not even have to leave their campus to have access to everything they could desire. And, when they do leave, the whole of New York is waiting for them.

One small note: although NYC provides nearly everything your heart can desire, it is not big on nature. If you feel the need to breathe fresh air and see the sky, your best bet is to get a bus or train and head for the wider world. The East Coast offers some great areas to hike, ski or sunbathe. Just remember, it is permissible to leave the island!

Getting In

While Columbia is known to be one of the least selective of the Ivy League schools, it is still one of the most popular universities in the United States. Approximately 11% of the students who apply to the college are accepted, 90% of whom were in the top 10% of their high-school class. Applicants should bear in mind that Columbia also offers some awesome combined programmes. If you are poised to become the next Jacqueline du Pré, you should remember that a joint programme with Juilliard is a possibility. And if you tend more towards engineering or science, it is possible to do combined degree courses.

All of these options require excellent grades. Columbia requests that everyone takes SAT Reasoning and then an additional two SAT IIs. More important than the exams, however, is the extent to which you show yourself to be a well-rounded and dedicated individual. Columbia is known for being a school that focuses as much on the person as on the grade and will count your school magazine/prefect/tutoring/generally being an all-round superstar as being just as valuable as a string of straight As. It is possible to interview with the Columbia graduates who are scattered around the world, but, if you can't set it up, it is not considered essential.

Columbia has embraced the age of technology and prefers that its applicants use the electronic application. They also offer the option of Early Decision applications but make sure that you're committed before you submit the form. If you're accepted, you have to go. For those who plan on taking the traditional English gap year, Columbia is very relaxed about deferment – provided you can prove you are actually doing something with the twelve months. Finally, although there is a certain amount of financial aid available, Columbia is not needs-blind for its international students.

Famous Grads

Allen Ginsberg and Jack Kerouac – Columbia defined the beat generation

Art Garfunkel – 'The Graduate'

Alfred Knopf – publishing magnate

And as for Barnard ...

Although it is a pretty safe bet that most English students, regardless of their education up to this point, are not too keen to lock themselves up in single-sex institutions for the next four years, it is worthwhile giving Barnard a mention. For all those girls out there who are looking for a top-rate education in the most exciting of American cities, this is a possible option. The female counterpart of the now co-ed Columbia, Barnard enjoys all of Columbia's facilities as well as its own, and is known as one of the strongest female colleges thriving in the United States today.

Each of Barnard's year groups consists of around 500 students – their only real similarity being their gender. Barnard prides itself on having a diverse community – incorporating every type of woman and providing them all with a place that allows them to go wherever they want. Strong communities of every type exist on campus, and, whether you are a party girl or a library fan, you'll be sure to find a home. Furthermore, and definitely owing to its gender composition, Barnard is known to be a very tolerant and politically active community. Thus, it has been able to accommodate groups as diverse as the strong gay community or the many Orthodox Jews who can be found on campus. This is part of Barnard's charm. Like the city in which it is situated, it embraces all ways of thinking and then simply gets on with the affairs in hand.

Perhaps the most important of these affairs is the education of its students. Barnard is extremely committed to ensuring that its students have the best of all worlds – including the academic. Barnard's special relationship with Columbia is extremely beneficial – students from both colleges can cross-register for any course they choose. And the fact that large numbers of Columbia students do flock to Barnard to learn from their expert faculty proves that this is a college that can compete with the best. Barnard students undertake distribution requirements specially designed to broaden their education as well as working closely with members of their chosen departments. And, at the end of four years, every senior must work towards some final thesis or product, the last hurdle that Barnard believes prepares them for the transition to the real world.

Barnard is not for everyone, and it is likely that many British girls (especially those who have suffered through years of single-sex education) may be turned off by the prospect of yet more female academia. Yet, for those who do consider this to be an option, Barnard offers a great and vibrant community, which, thanks to Columbia and the life of the surrounding area, also gives students a social life. Those who choose to go to Barnard (and it is an extremely competitive college) must take the SAT I and three SAT IIs (including writing). The place to shine, however, is the personal essay – an opportunity to show yourself to be the international, liberal and interesting person that everyone knows you are!

Famous Grads
Jhumpa Lahiri – hottest writer around
Joan Rivers – enough said
Martha Stewart – cooking and crime!

Cornell

Ithaca, New York
www.cornell.edu
13,700 undergraduates (4,400 Arts and Sciences), 20,225 graduates

How many students does it take to change a light bulb at Cornell? Two – one to change the light bulb and one to crack under the pressure.

When Ezra Cornell founded his Ivy League school in 1865, he gave it the motto – 'I would found an institution where any person can find instruction in any study'. His non-sectarian college was aimed at all people and catered for all interests. Cornell has taken this legacy and made it into one of the most thriving universities on the East Coast. Cornell, aka 'The Big Red', is the largest of the Ivy Leagues and allows you to study anything from agriculture to hotel management to the more conventional arts and sciences. This diverse academic experience takes place in one of the most naturally beautiful campuses in America. Cornell has none of the quaint and well-planned elements that define most New England campuses. Instead, its buildings are situated on a huge expanse of rural land, complete with rivers, waterfalls and acres and acres of parkland. For those looking for a fun campus life, great academics and the chance to go swimming in your very own gorge, Cornell is an appealing option.

The Campus

If you are a country bumpkin you will feel at home at Cornell University. The site was literally founded on Ezra Cornell's farm in 1865 and there is still a highly rated College of Agriculture for those who want to return to their rural roots. Even if you choose not to study the finer points of turnips, you will be surrounded by a natural beauty that you are simply not going to find at many universities in the US. The campus is situated on a hill overlooking Cayuga Lake and contains three gorges and many hiking paths. The hill means that, in the winters (which are invariably long and cold), all students get to try out their sledding skills on dining hall trays. And in the summers, the gorges (complete with waterfalls) provide an excellent place to cool off.

The actual Arts and Sciences campus is divided into two parts: the North Campus, which houses all the freshmen, creating a first-year bonding experience essential in such a large university; and the West Campus, which houses all the sophomores (except for those who choose to live with their frats). There are a total of thirty-three residential halls on campus, ranging from traditional Gothic styles to the less attractive modernist concrete. Juniors and seniors have a variety of housing options, dorms centred around a particular theme (international house, anyone?), university apartments in Collegetown, or their own choice of off-campus housing. The housing system provides pastoral care but also encourages independence – something that many students say is essential when they finally emerge into the real world.

The campus was laid out by Frederick Law Olmstead – the man who designed Central Park – and it has the same spacious, yet organized, feel. Despite its somewhat random position in what other schools like to label 'Middle of Nowhere, NY-State', Cornell has some architectural masterpieces of which students are rightly proud. Most famous of these is the McGraw clock tower which stands at the heart of the campus. Three times a day, teams of student chime-masters ascend the stairs and play the Alma Mater theme tune as well as a variety of other songs, including a selection of Beatles favourites. Other focal points on campus include Ho Square(!), where students petition, protest and generally hang out, the footbridge on Beebe Lake, which is meant to ensure marriage if you and your other half cross it holding hands, and the beautiful Uris Library, which houses one of the world's largest collections on witchcraft. Cornell also embraced the modern with the I. M. Pei-designed Johnson Museum of Art, one of the most interesting buildings on campus. Not only does it host art shows, concerts and other exhibitions, it also acts as a giant outdoor movie screen in the summer.

The Cornellian

As Ezra Cornell so proudly boasted, Cornell is a university where 'any person' can do pretty much anything. As a result it attracts a diverse student body. Cornell is the only Ivy League to be both a public and a private institution. While most of you will be heading for the private College of Arts and Science, the university has six other undergraduate schools. These are the College of Agriculture, College of Human Ecology, College of Industrial and Labour Relations, College of Engineering, School of Architecture, Art and Planning and the world-famous School of Hotel Administration (which supplies managers for hotels around the globe as well as running Cornell's own prestigious hotel). This mix of academic experience, and the fact that several of the colleges are state funded with lower tuition fees, ensure that Cornell draws a veritable mish-mash of people from every corner of America and far beyond.

One thing, however, links the Cornell community together – its school spirit. Regardless of the season, there are always thousands of students thronging the campus, of every conceivable background, ethnicity and religion. And nearly all of them will stop and extol its virtues. This love for the Alma Mater may be encouraged by the fact that, if you are stuck in the middle of nowhere for four years, you pretty much have to love your campus. Cornell undergrads feel passionately about 'The Big Red' and fiercely defend any insults levelled against the 'Bear' (their mascot) institution. There is a healthy sense of fun on the Cornell campus; something that is testified to by the large number of pranks that take place – most of them involving the hijacking of McGraw tower in some capacity.

When Cornell was initially founded, it was intended to be a university open to people of all religious persuasions. This legacy of tolerance and non-discrimination continues today. Cornell was the first American university to open a black fraternity and it continues to have a strong and well-integrated minority population (estimated at around 27%). It also has many privileged, privately educated white kids, many of whose parents attended Cornell back in their day. Although, as at all universities, students complain that certain groups like to self-segregate, it is generally agreed that Cornell students are both easy-going and accommodating. This is good news for crazy Brits who will benefit from slotting right into a diverse environment that is rarely found in England.

You will also have to adjust to the American impulse to take part in pretty much everything that is going on, all the time. The extra-curriculars at Cornell are exhaustive and exhausting. A typical day might begin with a volunteer programme in Ithaca, followed by some IM sport, then an article written at the Cornell *Daily Sun* (a higher-class publication than its name might suggest), followed by an evening tech rehearsal for the annual student production of the *Rocky Horror Show*. Somewhere in there you also have to fit three or four hours of class, a little studying, some food, a couple of hours of sleep, a bustling social life and, given that this is Cornell, a jog along the gorge. This may seem exhausting, but soon it becomes second nature and you can't imagine what you once did with all that free time.

Cornell is not for everyone. It is a huge school and, as such, it is easy to be lost in the crowd. Cornell students need to have a certain amount of resilience and the courage to promote themselves both academically and socially. It is Ivy League folklore that Cornell has the highest suicide rate of any of the colleges, something that is traditionally blamed on the gorges. This unfortunate hearsay may no longer be true, but Cornell does have a full advising system in place for those who feel lost. However, for Brits, it may also be the university that feels most like home from home. The fact that many of the older years live off-campus, coupled with the pub-like mentality of fraternity life, provides those longing for a little bit of British 'uni' life with a somewhat similar experience in America. And for those to whom this very mentality is anathema, the school spirit and diversity of Cornell ensures that almost all will find their own niche.

Hitting the Books

It is a standing joke among Ivy League students that Cornell undergrads get away with having to do absolutely no work. This is actually not true, and there are many far more serious contenders to this claim (for example, the 'we have no mandatory courses' Brown). Cornell students vociferously advertise the amount of work they do have – citing the three to four classes they attend each day as well as the dreaded prelim (aka mid-term) exams that take place two or three times each semester – in contrast to once a semester at other universities.

Cornell students are fortunate enough to have a huge range of courses (over 4,000). Students can take subjects offered outside their own school and design their major to suit their own personal interest. As a rule, members of the Cornell faculty are thought to be approachable and helpful to undergrads. One caveat: Cornell has a huge graduate school and this often becomes the centre of attention. Many undergrads complain about the fact that it is the graduate students who get the best housing, professors and resources while they are left out in the cold. One of the reasons behind this frustration may be resentment of the bureaucracy that defines Cornell. Your professors could be the nicest in the world, but it doesn't help you with the endless red tape that is involved in changing class, registration or navigating the advising system.

And while the size of Cornell provides a wide range of possible class options, it also means you are unlikely to get the professor–student intimacy that characterizes smaller institutions. This, of course, depends on you. If you are brave, go to your professor's office and ask for their advice and help – you will benefit. If you are sensible, look out for the smaller seminars, and try to take classes that number around fifty students – you will feel connected. If you are neither of these things, you may end up as one in a sea of bored faces in a class of over four hundred. Of course, sometimes it is fun to be one in a huge class. Cornell's Psych 101 is famous for enrolling over 2,000 students, and most who take it love it. And, when you are in a large class, professors will try to ensure that you meet with either them or one of their TAs (normally grad students) to discuss issues in much smaller groups. But you should be prepared for the fact that this is not a university choice that is going to offer you much in the way of one-to-one tutorial time, unless you learn to be responsible for your own academic actions.

Cornell does not require much from its students in the way of core classes. Freshmen have to take two writing seminars, which are available on a huge variety of topics and are designed to set you up for the rest of your college career. There is also a two-semester physical education requirement – following the American mindset that fitness is key to every happy life. However, if you are exercise phobic, fear not. These requirements can be filled by yoga or fly fishing! And, as a final piece of eccentricity, all students must pass a swim test before they are allowed to graduate – three laps of a pool swimming any stroke that takes your fancy. This relaxed attitude to rigorous academic requirements pretty much sums up the Cornellian attitude. If you want it, it's there, but the onus is on you to go and get it. If you don't want it, the hope is that you'll still manage to pick up a lot just by following the crowd.

Social Life

The Cornell College of Arts and Sciences is the largest in the Ivy League. When you combine it with the six other undergraduate schools on campus and the huge number of graduate students, you have a vast community of young adults living pretty much on their own in the middle of nowhere. It would be a sad testament to the Cornell student if this environment resulted in a boring social life. Fortunately for the reputation of the campus, it has not, and Cornell is a fun place to attend college.

The huge size of the student body undeniably contributes to this social atmosphere. In such a large group of people, virtually every taste has to be catered for. Therefore, whether you are interested in celebrating the Hindu festival of Diwali, a large event on campus, or in throwing fish at the Harvard ice hockey team during the annual match, you are sure to find a group of people who want to join in. Saturday nights on campus can involve anything from catching the latest screening at Cornell's very own cinema (anything from classic movies to foreign films to recent releases) to notching up a couple of bars in Collegetown before dancing the night away in one of the local clubs.

Cornell University is another of the colleges that embraces that curious American custom – the fraternity. It is estimated that around a third of the campus is involved in the Greek societies, with many of the sophomores actually living in their buildings. The college administration, fearful of drunken students and potential lawsuits, tries to maintain some control over the alcohol situation by insisting on university catering services, but most parties are still very much influenced by the heavy-drinking culture. This means that Cornell feels more like a big football school (despite the dubious status of its football team) than many of its East Coast contemporaries. In many ways your social experience here will be more like the average English pub culture than that at many of the more rarified American colleges. However, if you are not into keg stands and beer pong, you should rest assured that there are plenty of less hardcore options available to you and the many who share your reticence.

Outside Those Ivory Walls

Cornell, along with Dartmouth, has become the butt of many jokes for its less-than-perfect location. Harvard has Boston, Columbia has New York, Penn has Philadelphia ... when compared with these great cities, poor old Ithaca doesn't really have much of a look-in.

However, before you too succumb to the idea that Cornell is severely crippled by its geographical status, it is worth taking a closer look at the situation. While Ithaca may not be the biggest town in the world, it is a substantial one and offers pretty much every facility students may need. Unfortunately, if you are one of those people who *does* want to hit the metropolis on a regular basis, you are doomed to disappointment. New York City, while in the same state, is five hours away by car. Even getting to the university can be a problem for the international traveller – involving a flight into one of the New York City airports and then a local flight into Syracuse airport.

However, students looking for a little bit of excitement should not despair. The local and aptly named Collegetown, situated right next to the Cornell campus, provides a great place to hang out. Cornell is a huge university and thus there is a large student demand for all traditional amenities – entertainment, bars, clubs and coffee houses. Collegetown supplies all of these and is continually thronged by students who want a break from the on-campus frat scene. Cornell has a great social life and it really doesn't suffer from its location. In fact, visiting students who have to make do with the dubious delights of places such as Harvard Square are frequently envious of the bars, dance clubs and arcades that make up Collegetown. Furthermore, the fact that many juniors and seniors live off-campus allows for an entertaining feel (dinner and drinks parties) that hints at what real-world socializing may eventually be like.

In addition to these more social pursuits, Cornell also offers its students some of the most extensive outdoor benefits in the Ivy League. Surrounded by National Parks, it provides some great trails

for the enthusiastic hiker, one of which actually starts at the door of an on-campus dorm. In the winter, skiing is readily available as well as sledging and skating, and, in the summer, long walks through the Cornell Plantations and swims in the gorges are a popular choice. Even the most urbanite student will miss the natural beauty of the place at the end of their four years.

Getting In

Every year Cornell receives around 20,000 applications for 3,000 spots in its incoming freshman class. This is pretty tough going, but you should not be disheartened. Not only is Cornell the biggest Ivy League college (bigger = more spots), it also does not place as much weight on SAT scores as some of the others. Furthermore, it goes out of its way to offer international students a little leeway on their scores. Cornell requires that you take the SAT Reasoning and three SAT IIs. It also offers you the possibility of an alumni interview, something definitely recommended as it will give you an additional perspective on a place that you may only have visited briefly, if at all. Cornell also requires the normal application essay – in the format of a long essay. Questions follow the traditional American pattern of trying to get to the bottom of your personal belief system – some current examples include: 'What quotation or motto describes your values? What event has occurred in your life that was influenced by other perspectives? What question would you have liked us to have asked? Answer it'. It is this essay that really forms the heart of your application and it is important to put some serious consideration into how you answer it. Your application can be submitted either online or on paper (but don't forget to take into consideration the inevitable delays in the international postal service).

Cornell does now offer the Early Decision option to its applicants. Only do this if you are committed to attending 'The Big Red', because, if you are accepted, you must withdraw all applications to other schools. There is a small amount of financial aid available to international students, but it does not come in the guaranteed-to-all-who-really-need-it package of other schools. Therefore, if you are eager to pursue this route, you need to look into it as soon as possible.

Famous Grads

Christopher Reeve – what's good enough for Superman should be good enough for you
E. B. White – hooray for 'Charlotte's Web'!
Adolph Coors – if Coors beer isn't your favourite drink now, it soon will be

Dartmouth

Hanover, New Hampshire
www.dartmouth.edu
4,100 undergraduates, 1,100 graduates

How many students does it take to change a light bulb at Dartmouth?
None – Hanover doesn't have electricity.

Ever read 'The Cat in the Hat'? The creator of green eggs and ham hailed from Dartmouth, smallest of the eight Ivy League schools. Tucked away in a remote corner of New Hampshire, Dartmouth is not for those who seek the bright lights of the big cities. Yet for those seeking a university experience that allows them to travel, ski on their own slopes and assemble a wardrobe based around the colour green, while simultaneously exposing themselves to some of the best teaching around, Dartmouth is a top choice. After all, if it was good enough for Dr Seuss, what's stopping you?

The Campus

Dartmouth was founded in 1769 by the Rev. Eleazar Wheelock and was designed to educate Indian tribe children and the sons of the British. His mission was to spread Christian morals and beliefs from one to the other in an attempt to civilize the area. Hence, the school motto remains '*vox clamantis in deserto*' – a voice crying out in the wilderness. While New Hampshire is no longer the wilderness it once was, it is still not the most cosmopolitan place. However, what it lacks in urbanity, it makes up for in breathtaking beauty. Situated between the Vermont and New Hampshire mountains, Dartmouth students have the option of hiking on their own trails, skiing on their own slopes and skating on their own pond; certainly not something that England can offer.

The Dartmouth campus is situated around the Green, initially an area used for herding cattle and now populated by sprawling students in the summer and snowballing students in the winter. The Green is also the site for some of the more pagan of the school's festivities – bonfires for fall Homecoming, ice sculptures (yes, it is this cold) for the Winter Carnival and all manner of celebrations for the spring Green Key. Dotted around the Green are the main residential buildings and classrooms of the campus. Many of them are in classic New England fashion (think red brick, white spires) – most notably the beautiful Baker Library. There are, however, some more modern additions, including the 'Hop' or Hopkins Center for the Arts – the performance centre on campus.

The Dartmouth Student

Dartmouth has been labelled the 'country club' of the Ivy Leagues – a reputation that is not altogether undeserved. The combination of a small and elite university, catering to intelligent and elite students in beautiful and elite surroundings, does suggest a certain exclusive quality. Despite the original vision of an Indian/English school – catering to all nationalities and cultures – diversity has been a serious problem at Dartmouth. While this issue has lessened in recent years – 32% of students are now from ethnic minorities – students still report a certain amount of segregation between different racial groups. The situation is constantly improving, but Dartmouth has found it difficult to shrug off its legacy of white privilege.

The average Brit will not, however, be much affected by this. The student body is large enough to encompass all friendship groups, and Dartmouth prides itself on a sense of community. As long as you are open with everyone, everyone will be open with you. In many senses the Dartmouth atmosphere bears much resemblance to that of a British uni. If you are feeling homesick, there is tea served every day at four (faculty and students welcome). Even more importantly for those used to non-Draconian drinking laws, the campus has its own pub – The Lone Pine Tavern – a rare institution at American universities and one seemingly designed to make the Brit feel at home.

In fact, Dartmouth as a whole is an extremely friendly place. Although there are graduate schools, these students are outnumbered by the undergrads at a rate of four to one. The number of young people and the isolated position of the school ensure a close-knit campus community that bonds over the cold, the colour green and the delights of having accommodation with working fireplaces. 85% of students choose to live on campus, in the attractive buildings situated around the Green. Some of these are themed houses (international, substance-free, etc.), but most combine all year groups, majors and ethnicities for a diverse living experience. And most students eat together in the nationally renowned dining halls – forget the cafeteria experience, this food is really good.

The life of the average Dartmouth student is very much defined by the unique D-Plan or semester schedule. Any Brit who comes to the US is bound to be perplexed by the term system that universities have. While most colleges divide the year in two, cutting out Easter holiday and focusing instead on the summer, Dartmouth offers an entirely different solution. They split each year up into seasons (yes, there are actually seasons in New Hampshire). The student then has a choice as to where to spend the four ten-week terms. It is obligatory to be on campus for the first three of both freshman and senior year and for the summer term of your sophomore year. But you can then also choose to study off-campus – either abroad or in some form of internship – for as many as three other terms. Confused? The Dartmouth website explains all this brilliantly – even allowing you to plot your own academic schedule for the next four years.

This D-Plan system means that Dartmouth students are constantly on the move. While this can be disruptive, it also means that you are continually being exposed to new people and new ideas. Even the potentially off-putting notion of a summer spent at school is actually much loved by the student body who devote most of it to sunbathing and lazing around with friends. Dartmouth students pride themselves on their sense of community. From the first days on campus, when everyone is hooked up to the much-famed Blitz email network, to the regular alumni events and large turnout at sports events, the Dartmouth student body moves as a pack and is proud to do so.

Despite its alienated position and relatively small endowment, Dartmouth has pretty much every resource you can think of. And students don't hesitate to use them. There are a plethora of clubs and societies on campus, and everyone gets involved with something. Whether you are writing for *The Dartmouth* (one of many papers that claims to be the oldest college publication) or doing research at the hospital of the prestigious Dartmouth Med. School, your days will be busy. And, if you have a free moment, you can always go to watch the fruits of someone else's labour – performances of every variety abound.

Hitting the Books

Dartmouth is known for having one of the most dedicated faculties in the country, and students cannot sing their praises loud enough. Perhaps it is because the community is fairly small, or perhaps it is because New Hampshire just attracts a better brand of professor. Whatever the reasons, undergrads never feel neglected. They are the primary focus on campus and they feel the benefits. The class sizes are very small, professors are required to teach undergrads and the relationships formed in an academic setting often extend well beyond the classroom. As a result, students seldom feel alienated or lost regarding their academic well-being and, if they do, advisers who actually care are always on hand. It is hardly surprising that Dartmouth continually ranks top for teaching in a variety of nation-wide league tables.

Dartmouth offers over 2,000 courses in twenty-nine departments – a huge amount of flexibility complemented by the fact that no one has to choose a major until the end of sophomore year. Eventually, only about a third of your study while at university will be in your major. The rest will be taken up by exploring your own personal interests and by the Dartmouth equivalent of a core curriculum. Their liberal arts programme for undergraduates encompasses ten courses taken across eight different intellectual fields and requires that students immerse themselves in three different cultures (American, European and Non-Western).

Dartmouth also prides itself on the cosmopolitan atmosphere on campus. Over 50% of its students study abroad, and everyone is required to pass a language requirement. In fact, a French profes-sor, Prof. Rassais, developed a new system of teaching languages that is now widely followed – in addition to normal classes, students are required to meet once a day (often at 7.30am) and be drilled in grammar and vocabulary. This unique style of teaching indicates the energy that faculty members put into their duties at Dartmouth – energy from which the students benefit.

While Dartmouth may be isolated, it has every academic resource that the overeager undergraduate could desire. From the oldest research library in the country (the dreaming spired Baker Library) to the labs at the famous med. school, Dartmouth students have it all at their fingertips. And they are continually encouraged to use it. The D-Plan means that students are encouraged to seek out what appeals to them – whether it involves archaeological digs or an internship at Goldman Sachs. Academics are important, but only in so far as they serve the overall picture – flexibility and personal interest are prized above all else.

Before everyone decides that Dartmouth is the only place to go, one warning should be given. The past couple of years have seen a number of upheavals on the otherwise idyllic campus and an admin-istration–student schism has become most apparent. Whether in the battle over frats or the administration's desire to cut back on some of Dartmouth's most individual characteristics, students have been complaining that their unique university is under siege from within. Much of this is in the process of being resolved, but the atmosphere remains somewhat strained and there may well be more changes in the imminent future.

Social Life

It's Saturday night. It's cold. You're surrounded by mountains. The nearest city is two and half hours away. What do you do with yourself? Surprisingly, many Dartmouth students have been able to come up with fun and satisfying answers to this question. Despite its situation, Dartmouth students enjoy a social life that others at better-connected schools might well envy. While there may not be the plethora of locations that big cities offer, Hanover has enough restaurants to keep the students happy and there is always a large amount going on back at the campus.

Dartmouth is known for having a stronger drinking culture than many American universities – although it still pales into insignificance besides places such as Newcastle! This may well be due to the fact that frats still (despite the controversial efforts of the administration) play a large part in on-campus social life. (Of course, it may also be due to the fact that there isn't that much else to do, but this goes down less well with the average Dartmouth man.) Anyway, 37% of students choose to be affiliated with one of the fourteen fraternities and eight sororities (as well as three co-eds) that exist on campus. Although this may all seem a little bit too like a scary American movie to you – these organizations really do serve to spice up student social life and offer an alternative group of friends. In an effort to ensure that the campus is not totally dominated by these Greek groups, no freshmen are allowed into parties (generally open to everyone else on campus) in the first term, and rush (the process of selecting or being selected) does not take place until the sophomore winter term. This may seem a little unfair to overeager first years, but it does ensure that everyone has a chance to get to know each other in a situation that is not dependent on which Greek initials you sport on your jumper.

One caveat: students at most Ivy League schools complain that romance is dead, dating a thing of the past and true love something that is only found when taking a class on *Romeo and Juliet*. While a lot of this is mere griping, it is true that the whirl of an American student's daily life leaves little time for relationships. At Dartmouth this is complicated by the D-Plan. Students are constantly moving around on campus, and it can be difficult to develop a short-term hook-up into a long-term romance when one or both partners are jetting off to pastures new for the next semester; something for the relationship junkies to bear in mind.

Outside Those Ivory Walls

If you enjoyed *The Sound of Music* as a child, then you will feel very at home at Dartmouth. While the mountains of Vermont and New Hampshire may not be quite as impressive as the Alps, they still form a pretty imposing backdrop to your daily life. Unfortunately for those who prefer shopping to sledding and clubbing to climbing, Dartmouth does not have as much to offer. While the town of Hanover is pretty and enjoys an extremely close relationship to the university, it is also small and can really only offer students a momentary escape from campus life.

However, those students who choose to go to Dartmouth firmly believe that the limited options available to them help form a close community. While Hanover has sufficient restaurants, coffee houses and entertainment to suit those who crave a world off the Green, the campus society itself provides a multitude of entertainments. Dartmouth students make their own fun, and the combination of frats, obscure school traditions and community atmosphere means that there is rarely a dull moment. And for those who need an urban fix once in a while, Lebanon airport offers daily flights to both New York City and Boston – which if you are one of the few who have a car is only a three-hour drive.

What Dartmouth lacks in urban entertainment, it makes up for in rural pursuits. This is not the sort of place where a hatred of the outdoors will get you very far. Almost all incoming freshmen participate in an introductory hiking programme designed to accelerate the bonding experience so favoured in America. While not everyone would choose to meet their friends for the next four years in an atmosphere defined by tents and tinned food, many find it a good way to break down initial social barriers. And everyone is in agreement that the surrounding countryside is gorgeous. Hiking continues to play an integral role in the lives of many students, and, for those who prefer more glamorous pursuits, the long winter provides ample opportunity for hitting the fourteen-trail Dartmouth ski mountain!

Getting In

Dartmouth is not the kind of place that people put on their application list as a fall back. The students who decide to apply there are determined and ever increasing in number. Around 20% of applications are accepted (roughly 2,000 out of the 10,000 or so who apply annually). And most of these students have SAT scores above 1400. While Dartmouth does not place emphasis on academics alone, a strong background is needed if you are to succeed.

Dartmouth requires the customary SAT I and three SAT IIs – although it does go out of its way to state that it understands that international students may be at a disadvantage. It also offers the possibility of an alumni interview – a forum that allows the school to question you and, more importantly, you to question the school. Many American graduates are based in the UK and it is normally possible to locate one relatively close to you. If you cannot, it will in no way count against you.

As well as official academic reports and the more revealing interview information, Dartmouth also asks for letters that champion your cause. In addition to the guidance counsellor/school principal and teacher reports that most universities seek, Dartmouth also places importance on a peer letter – written about you by one of our friends. So it may pay off to start being really nice to people NOW! Dartmouth is an expensive university and it does not offer needs-blind admission to its international students. However, those who need financial aid should not despair – Dartmouth is normally able to meet this need when it is demonstrated. Lastly, you can apply to Dartmouth on an Early or a Regular Decision basis. Remember, Early Decision is binding so it is important to be sure before you send in that envelope.

Famous Grads

Robert Frost – great American poet

Dr Seuss (Theodore Geisel) – 'Cat in the Hat', 'Green Eggs and Ham' ...

Nelson Rockefeller – VP and millionaire

Duke

Durham, North Carolina
www.duke.edu
6,500 undergraduates, 6,200 graduates

How many students does it take to change a light bulb at Duke?
A whole frat – but only one of them is sober enough to get the bulb
out of the socket.

Duke University's reputation has been on the rise over the last few
years. And rightly so. Once dismissed as a mere prep school contin-
uation for the Southern elite, this beautiful college, set in the heart
of the South, has now established itself as an academic and sporting
success drawing students from all over the nation. If you are a basketball fanatic, a lover of the South, longing to join a fraternity,
dying for some warm weather or merely in search of a US education
that avoids the East Coast stereotypes, then Duke is well worth your
consideration. Duke offers a highly social campus set a mere fifteen
minutes away from other top Southern schools (Chapel Hill among
them) as well as great academics and a thriving school spirit. After
all, who wouldn't want to be known as a Blue Devil?

The Duke campuses are famed for their beautiful architecture,
lovely grounds and wonderful climate. They are also famed for the
fact that there are two of them. Students love to bitch about the division that this sets up – although they are, in fact, connected by bus
or a short walk. Indeed, for many, the combination acts as an advantage. Not only aesthetically – East Campus is the older of the two,
complete with Georgian architecture, while West Campus epito-
mizes the Gothic style, topped off by the soaring Duke Chapel – but
also socially. Freshmen all live on the East Campus, allowing for a
mass bonding experience. Upperclassmen live on the West Campus
– a transition that lets them leave the frenetic pack socializing of

freshman year behind and settle down in their own fraternities or smaller residential halls. The fact that 90% of Duke students choose to live on campus suggests that the groans about the division of the two sites are really just because there isn't much else to moan about. The Blue Devils are known for being a friendly lot and, while the university has expanded far beyond its Southern roots, a great deal of the Southern charm remains. Admittedly this emphasis on manners (which English students will find not dissimilar to that back home) comes with other qualities that can be more daunting. Girls on the Duke campus should expect to be always impeccably turned out, while boys should be prepared to embrace the frat house scene and join the drunken revelry of the blue-blooded and conservative elites. Many claim that Duke is a superficial place that, despite its attempts at diversity, has been unable to fully shake off its 'little rich boy' image. Others, however, state that it is easy to get beyond these initial stereotypes and that the campus is becoming ever more diverse and tolerant for those who do not believe in cocktail parties and little black dresses.

One thing that brings together the entire student body is the craze for the Duke basketball team. Even if you have no conception of this game beyond a hazy association with netball, you will soon find yourself joining the ranks of Blue Devils who stalk members of the top national team around campus and live in tents for weeks in order to get game tickets. Nor does this enthusiasm for their campus stop on the sports fields. Duke students are keen to join everything – among the many groups on campus are the top improv troupe in the country, a strong student newspaper and a good arts programme.

Duke likes to be known as a party school, and the frat scene ensures there is seldom a dull Saturday night. But students also take pride in their academics, and many believe that it is their will to work that is pushing Duke up the college rankings. Certainly, the faculty is excellent and more than willing to put in the man-hours to secure personal interaction with their students. While it may be difficult at first to find the intellectual environment that suits you (especially with so many other students), the sheer number of courses coupled with an inquisitive spirit will ensure that you discover your place. Students find themselves facing a rigorous core curriculum, ensuring they graduate as well-rounded individuals who are fluent in basic maths as well as Shakespearean sonnets. But they also have two years to decide what major to pursue and the option of pursuing more than one if they simply can't make up their minds.

Duke students like to boast that Harvard is the 'Duke of the North', and certainly their academic strength is ensuring them a premier reputation. Despite the large number of grad students, Duke maintains a healthy focus on the undergraduate. Its freshmen seminars and focus groups ensure that even the babies of the college feel they are getting enough attention. The Duke administration has also recently won itself instant popularity by giving all freshmen a free iPod to enhance their access to certain courses (and their ability to download the latest Britney!). No one knows if this scheme will be repeated (some are worried that it stunts social interactions), but it demonstrates the healthy nature of the relationship between student and college.

And after the halcyon days of college are left behind, students go on to hugely successful careers across the board. Duke boasts of a 99% acceptance rating for those of its students heading to law school, and an 80% rating for those looking at medicine. Certainly, the enthusiasm and confidence of the average Devil gives them a boost in the job market. If all of this sounds like a good option for you, then heading to North Carolina (itself an experience) to take a look around is highly recommended. Make sure you chat with a Blue Devil Advocate – these student tour leaders are renowned for being both honest and highly persuasive! And sign yourself up for your SATs now, the usual SAT Reasoning and two SAT IIs (a foreign language one comes highly recommended).

Famous Grads
Richard Nixon – President of the USA
Melinda Gates – husband Bill is a more than generous donor
Anne Tyler – writer

Georgetown

Georgetown, Washington, DC
www.georgetown.edu
6,000 undergraduates, 5,400 graduates

How many students does it to take to change a light bulb at Georgetown?
Four – one to change it, one to call Congress about their progress, and two to throw the old bulb at the American U. students.

Georgetown is one of the few universities in America where international students blend right in. This Jesuit college was founded in 1789 in Washington, DC and has remained a thriving institution for the last three hundred years. Located a stone's throw away from the centre of American government, it has an informed and politicized scholastic environment. It also has a Foreign Service school which surprisingly, given America's frequently insular attitude to the rest of the world, actually advocates the merits of being able to locate Europe on a map and is known for being the best of its kind. As a result of this internationalist atmosphere, foreign students head to Georgetown in droves. And why not? After all, what's good enough for Bill Clinton should be good enough for you.

The Campus

The founders of Georgetown did a pretty good job picking out their site – situated on a hill, overlooking the Potomac River, in the middle of the nation's capital, the campus' location could not be better. The buildings, on the other hand, are a mixed bag – some pretty architecture and a great deal of modern work that leaves a little to be desired. However, while it may lack the quaint, dreaming spires feel of the New England campus, Georgetown has the bustling feel of a university in a big city and a surprising amount of its own space. (As a side-note to all of those anxious parents, it is also situated in one of the safest parts of the notoriously crime-ridden DC.)

The surrounding area is also one of the prettiest and most historic in town – old brick housing on streets that are conveniently named after letters of the alphabet. Although the metro system is a little unreliable in this part of DC, it is an easy bus ride into the centre of a city that (as befits a capital) always has something going on. DC, unlike New York, has a fairly relaxed atmosphere and a much nicer climate (except for in those humid summer months when you remember it is a city built on a bog). And for those students who want to escape the big city, there are plenty of open parkland spaces designed to make the Londoner feel at home.

The Student Body

Perhaps because of its political connections and prime real estate position in one of the more exclusive parts of Washington, Georgetown has always had a reputation for drawing in rich, white, prepschool kids – the inevitable step between Philips Exeter and a seat in Congress. It also appeals to educationally minded Europeans (more serious Brown types) who flock to the excellent School of Foreign Service. Yet, despite these crowds of international students all over campus, students have traditionally complained about the lack of any real ethnic or religious diversity. In recent years this trend has thankfully been reversed, but WASPy cliques with a strong elitist attitude are still very much a presence on campus – and tend to look fondly on the class-conscious Brit.

Georgetown remains a Jesuit university and a strong Catholic presence still thrives on campus. It is estimated that approximately 50% of the students are Catholic. While religious tension is seldom part of the everyday environment, some non-Catholic students have complained that, at least in the initial months, they feel very much in the minority. Religious traditions, such as the refusal of the campus medical system to provide the birth control pill, are subjects of strong debate. Most students, however, agree that the campus is both large and diverse enough to accommodate any belief system or political opinion. The Hoyas (as Georgetown students like to refer to themselves) are a pretty friendly bunch, and the fact they frequently aspire to future political office means they are only too happy to practise both their people skills and their international diplomacy! All of the freshmen on campus live together in dorms, and, by the time people move onto their next three years of housing, many of the initial barriers have been broken down and bonds formed across every divide, religious and otherwise.

The student body at Georgetown is, as one might expect from a politically savvy group of young adults, extremely active. Many of these kids are in training for a campaign trail or podium speech, and there are always a hundred and one things going on. Whether you choose to get involved in social programmes (parts of DC are among the poorest in America), political organizations or the omnipresent sports teams, you can expect to have a good part of each day taken up by those extra-curricular activities that many Brits are too busy lazing in the pub ever to get around to doing. Students here also tend to be from fairly prosperous classes – and there are a lot of rich and ambitious individuals around. Be warned – people here take their position in life, and their future advancement, extremely seriously.

Hitting the Books

The Georgetown campus is made up of four undergraduate schools – the School of Foreign Service (SFS) and the School of Arts and Sciences (where most students would be headed) and then the School of Business and the School of Nursing. As a prospective student, you apply to and are accepted by a particular school. Once you are on campus, however, any undergraduate is able to take classes at any of the other colleges. Each school also imposes a liberal arts core curriculum upon its students – ensuring that its nurses can quote Shakespeare as well as sew up wounds and its diplomats can balance their chequebooks at the end of the year. The SFS cannot come highly recommended enough – with a wonderful curriculum, great travel options and a premier academic reputation – it is the place to start if you are looking for an ambassadorship someday!

Despite their curricula requirements, Georgetown students are more than enthusiastic about both their class loads and their professors. Although class sizes are sometimes a little bigger than the ideal, smaller sections, office hours and informal meetings ensure that students get more than enough time with their teachers. Political students are particularly turned on by the Georgetown environment – many of their professors are also employees of the political administration and classes often feature surprise appearances by congressmen or senators. Internships on the Hill are also a possibility for the very lucky – or politically savvy. If your interests fall more towards saving humanity than accumulating power, the local NGOs (mostly situated in Dupont Circle) also offer internships aplenty, while internationalists can take refuge at the lines of embassies that pop up all over DC.

Social Life

If you are the type of student who looks forward to spending four years doing keg stands and joining fraternities with names like

Kappa Kappa Delta Phi, then Georgetown is not the place for you. But, despite not having a Greek scene, there are more than enough parties and events for everybody else. The campus itself has certain annual rituals – where else in the country could you attend an undergraduate Diplomats Ball? – that are always packed with people. And when on-campus casino nights get too much for you, DC offers a plethora of other options. The Georgetown area itself is home to some very cool bars, nice (although expensive) restaurants and fun clubs. And, for those seeking a bustling but more studenty nightlife, the Adams Morgan area (famous for being the place where underage presidential twins came to grief) offers streets of fun Saturday night options.

Getting In

Unsurprisingly, the nationally renowned standards of Georgetown make this an increasingly competitive place to be admitted to. Around 15,000 students apply each year for only 1,500 places – a ratio of 10:1 which is more than a little daunting. Although you might have a slight edge as an international student, a strong application is essential. Georgetown requires three SAT IIs and the SAT I as well as a pre-entrance interview. The interview is mandatory and there are alumni situated in London and other places in the UK who are only too happy to make sure you are the right kind of person to do honour to their Alma Mater. Sell yourself to them, but also make sure they sell the place to you – getting the inside scoop is all-important in choosing the right place for you to spend the next four years of your life. And be warned, while Georgetown does have a few financial aids packages for international students, you have to ask for them and needs-blind admission is not an option.

Famous Grads

Bill Clinton – statesman extraordinaire, need we say more?
Felipe de Borbon – Crown Prince of Spain
George Tenet – former CIA chief

Harvard

Cambridge, Massachusetts
www.harvard.edu
6,500 undergraduates, 12,000 graduates

How many students does it take to change a light bulb at Harvard?
One – he holds the bulb and the world revolves around him.

You can always spot the English people who get into Harvard. Ask
them where they're going to university and they'll somewhat shiftily
reply, 'America'. Ask them where in America and they'll say,
'Somewhere in Boston'. Pry further and you'll eventually be rewarded by a combination of pride, humility and general embarrassment
as they mumble, 'Harvard'. This false modesty is rewarded in
England because Harvard is about the only American university that
anyone over here has ever heard of. The oldest university in
America, it also (rightly) prides itself on being one of the greatest.
From its early beginnings to the latest league rankings, Harvard has
stayed at the head of the field – a name that carries worldwide recognition. With faculty that dominate international academia, a mere
22 billion dollar endowment to play with and alumni who sing its
praises across the globe, Harvard is definitely one option that you
want to leave on your list.

The Campus
Harvard's campus is akin to that of so many of the other big New
England universities – a mix of charming old and fairly revolting
new. Of course, Harvard, founded in 1636, revels in the fact that its
old is older than anyone else's and its new, while almost universally
disliked, was designed by architects such as Le Corbusier. The campus centres around the 'Yard'. This attractive expanse of green,
enclosed by red brick buildings, plays host to the oldest dorm rooms

(once used to house troops fighting the British), the magnificent Widener Library, the striking memorial church and throngs of students tossing Frisbees, sunbathing, snowballing or participating in the biannual naked run! Freshmen enjoy all the advantages of living in this heart of the college campus, placed in smaller houses with more supervision and more exposure to their year group than the older classes.

The extended Harvard campus consists of a collection of houses (modelled on Oxbridge colleges) where the upper-class students live. Some of these bear the good old New England names of their Puritan founders (Eliot, Winthrop, Kirkland and Lowell) and have changed little since the eighteenth century. However, the housing lottery can be cruel and other students find themselves relegated to the old Radcliffe quad with its modern monstrosities and long walk from the central campus. Inevitably, each house develops its own sense of camaraderie, and people grow to love even the ugliest dorms. In addition, the advantage of en masse freshman housing means that initial bonds often last entire university careers. Thus, the disadvantages of being housed nearer to Canada than the Yard are softened somewhat by the fact that friendship groups are dispersed all over.

Many students gripe about the Harvard campus and its accommodation. The noisy Mass. Avenue cuts straight past the Yard and ruins the tranquil feel that John Harvard initially aimed for, while Harvard Square has sacrificed much of its eclectic intellectual charm and succumbed to big brand name shops. Students also consistently moan about being crammed into rooms with little space or privacy. In American colleges it is not unusual to find yourself with a roommate for some of your four years, something that rarely occurs on this side of the pond. At Harvard, however, divine recompense ensures that those houses that are attractive and central generally offer much worse accommodation than those that are modern and isolated. And moan as they may, most students would probably agree that your room serves as little more than a base from which to conduct the rest of your frenetic life. Similarly, although Harvard has, like all modern universities, had to lose some of its olde worlde charm, it remains a vibrant and attractive place in which the vast majority of students are proud to live.

The Crimson Man/Woman

Whatever else you can say to insult them, Harvard students are never ones to be left behind. Most of them are used to being the best in their high schools, and the combination of all of these IQs (and egos) in a high-pressure, academic environment often leads to some explosive results. It is said that every year Harvard would be able to fill its freshman class with people who have achieved 100% on every SAT exam they took. It speaks highly of Harvard that they try to look beyond that and gather together a group of people whose talents go beyond the rigorously intellectual. And they get what they want. Harvard has, and always has had, the highest yield rate among its applicants, a statistic that suggests it is near impossible to turn down. After all, author bias aside, Harvard is Harvard.

Arriving at Harvard can be a rather daunting experience. You may well find yourself sharing a room with a concert pianist or eating with someone who has already won two Olympic medals. This is one of the most valuable parts of the Harvard experience. Every individual there is interesting and talented – you just have to take a deep breath and remind yourself that the admissions committee can't have screwed up that badly picking you. (Harvard lore has it that most students spend their freshman year asking, 'How did I get here?', and their sophomore year wondering, 'How did you get here?' – so don't be too nervous those first few days.) Just remember, everyone is there for a reason – and that reason doesn't have to be an ability to make straight As.

Inevitably, all these brain cells and talent can lead to a competitive and ultrafocused environment. People at Harvard are always stressed out and (like every other elite school in the country) enjoy nothing more than moaning about how much more work they have than anyone else in the entire world. While the problems of adjusting to the strains of a bigger workload and new social environment mean that some freshmen can have a tricky time, most people quickly settle down. And, by their second year, students have easily learnt how to juggle the bare minimum of work with the maximum amount of free time. After that, the moans simply become another status symbol!

Harvard students always like to be protesting about something. If they're not bemoaning the latest curricular changes, they're launching a living wage campaign against the university administration. Grumbling about grades is only one minor indication of a valuable desire to get involved and change things. Harvard students love participation, and no day is complete without a mind-boggling range of extracurricular activities. Whether they are organizing marches on University Hall, writing a weekly column for the renowned daily *Crimson* or involved in a social-service scheme that benefits half of Boston, there are few Harvard students who spend all their free time in bed. With well-respected orchestras, choirs and drama troupes, not to mention the numerous sports teams, Harvard offers something for almost everyone, and most people are only too keen to pursue an extra hobby (or seven!)

Harvard students like to revel in their tradition and history, but are also keen to point out that the university has come a long way from the rich, white man ethos that defined it for hundreds of years. This is not to say that Lowells, Winthrops, Cabots and a handful of other Mayfloweresque names do not still haunt the campus. The traditions of these East Coast elite continue to thrive, but an influx of international and minority students has diluted them. The problem for the future lies in integrating these groups. Many Harvard students complain that self-segregation means that the student body (while apparently diverse) is still fairly socially homogenous. But the average English student (themselves a token diversity point for Harvard) will encounter more varied ethnic, religious and political backgrounds in one day of this university than in their entire high school career.

Almost everyone eventually discovers that Harvard students are friendly, enthusiastic and easy to get to know. The fact that the university boasts the largest endowment of any in America points to the commitment and affection of its alumni. It is also vital in ensuring that Harvard students are spoilt rotten. Money can be wheedled out of the university for just about any purpose, whether your desire is to set up a tiddlywinks club or to get a grant to go and study the beers of Bratislava. And once you have your grant, you'll almost certainly discover a student who has done the very same thing before and a top-notch faculty member who is keen to support you.

Hitting the Books

Words cannot describe the calibre of some of the Harvard faculty. This is an institution that regularly recruits the best brains in the world, seducing them to Cambridge with promises of tenure and academic glory and then plonking them down in front of a class of undergrads. While the best brains in the world might resent such treatment, the undergrads benefit hugely and the teaching resources at Harvard are truly the thing that make it one of the world's best universities. Harvard has first-class academic resources – from the vast Widener Library (beware, it is so huge you can lose mobile reception and be gone forever) to the incredible science labs, and all of them are available to the eager undergrad.

One of the more amazing things about Harvard (and there are many) is the fact that you are continually brushing shoulders with the gods of academia. Students really do see Seamus Heaney drinking in the local bar or Michael Sandel running late for class. Meanwhile, the pull of the H-bomb (or Harvard name) brings in speakers that range from Bill Clinton to Ali G. Professor–student interaction and contact with these big names is much encouraged, and faculty members could not be friendlier. All students need to do is screw up the courage to have a conversation with them and select their classes carefully. If you pick wisely and listen to people around you, you could end up in a seminar with someone as illustrious as President Summers himself.

Harvard students quickly learn the importance of never taking no for an answer. There is a renowned story about a professor who rejected all 200 of the applicants for a fifteen-place seminar and then accepted everyone who complained. The American university has no place in it for British manners and reserved modesty. There are numerous services and tutors who are more than willing to look out for you, but you have to ask them to do so. Go to office hours, talk to your professors (after all, how scary can a Nobel Prize winner or poet laureate be?), think about your courses and you will come out as the educated graduate your parents always hoped you would be.

Harvard's course load is fairly structured and can be extremely hard work. Those individuals who wish to spend four years in a pub, and believe that Widener Library is merely a place with great tobogganing opportunities when it snows, should think about whether Harvard is really the right place for them. Freshmen must declare a major (or concentration in Harvard-speak) at the end of their first year, much earlier than at other universities. Some of the departments do allow you an easy ride of it, but others have masses of requirements that can overburden even the most dedicated geek. Luckily, there are plenty of people (including your subject tutor) who can help you find the right balance. And once you've found your interest, you can be secure in the knowledge that almost nowhere else in the country will be able to offer you quite the same level of research facilities, labs and general guidance (thanks to those 22 billion dollars).

At the moment, Harvard's requirements are undergoing a prolonged review. Many students are busy crossing their fingers and praying that the eventual result will do away with the dreaded core curriculum. In fact, it seems likely that the core (which accounts for a quarter of the average course load) will become more rigorous. No student is going to be able to escape from compulsory science or maths – unless, of course, they are a maths major, and then they face compulsory poetry. Although students love to grumble about the core, many of the classes are in fact fairly easy-going – popular 'guts' include courses on dinosaurs and fairytales! In addition, core classes tend to be huge and more of a social and mind-expanding experience than a hard-core academic challenge.

Social Life
While Harvard tries its hardest, it has never really been able to shake off its 'put forty geeks in a room and you get a really bad party' image. Students still look back to its brief heyday in the swinging sixties, while Yalies mock from their more social campus. But while students may have to work a lot harder than their English peers to discover what's going on come Saturday night, there are plenty of social opportunities out there for those who want them. Freshmen may find themselves caught in an eternal cycle of dorm room cruising and the inevitable (puritan Massachusetts has no mercy) ID problem, but by the second year most students have established a social niche. Sports teams can normally be relied upon for the infamous keg parties, while the slightly more civilized head for the

plethora of restaurants and bars that Cambridge has to offer. The even more adventurous also have the option of the Boston club scene – Lansdowne Street offers a million club venues – where the whole university decamps for college parties on a fairly regular basis. Harvard also hosts that strange institution – the finals club. These male-only buildings, scattered around the Harvard campus, offer another refuge to the socially intrepid on a weekend night. Boys should, however, beware. As freshmen they stand as much chance of getting into one as a snowball does in hell (unless of course you have a contact on the inside). The 'Punch' (or recruiting) process takes place over sophomore year and allows each club to self-select its members for the next three years. Each club has a distinctive character (ranging from the WASPy Porc to the Eurotrashy Spee), and they offer a great place to go and party outside university jurisdiction. Girls, however, are frequently heard to complain that the atmosphere can be more like a meat market than socially enjoyable. Much debate is ongoing as to whether these undeniably elitist clubs are beneficial or detrimental to Harvard's image, but Brits seem to love them and no one can deny they throw some great parties!

Outside Those Ivory Walls

Cambridge itself is merely a suburb of Boston, but, to hear most Harvard students talk, you would think it was a self-contained town in the middle of nowhere. Although eager freshmen come to Harvard keen to experience life in a big city, many find that they rarely venture beyond the boundaries of Harvard Square. For those who do, and it is strongly recommended that you at least try, a whole new world opens up. Boston is a wonderful city (commonly believed to have the greatest number of affluent young singles in America) and packed with students. Whether you like clubbing, marathons, Italian pastries or ducklings, Boston is the place for you. A mere ten minutes by the famous T (underground) or a slightly longer and much more expensive cab ride, Boston is one of Harvard's best and most underused resources.

If your tastes lean more towards nature than Newbury Street (Boston's equivalent of 5th Avenue), then Harvard also allows for a certain amount of travelling. In the winter, if you are dedicated enough to battle through the inevitable snow, there are ski resorts close enough for weekend trips if you are lucky enough to have a friend with a car. In the warmer months, the wonderful Cape and Martha's Vineyard are reachable by bus. Meanwhile, opportunities for hiking, sailing and all those other outdoorsy things abound.

Finally, for those who find Boston too limited (which is pretty hard given its size and diversity), New York is near enough for a weekend visit. About four hours by car or one hour by the wonderful air shuttle, it offers a great alternative for those who crave the amusements of the biggest city of them all.

Getting In

Harvard takes a certain amount of pride in boasting about the number of immensely talented and academically superior students that it rejects each year. This can be somewhat disheartening to the already nervous applicant. But while there can be no doubt that Harvard demands your highest grades and maximum academic effort, it also values those other random things that make up such a diversely amazing student body. So speak out to them about your record for the 100 m or your early years in outer Mongolia. If they went for grades alone, they would have a pretty boring freshman class, and it's your job to show the other side to your character. The big chance to do this is in your admissions essay. The more random the subject and the more passionate you are about it, the better you will do.

On a more factual level, Harvard demands the standard SAT I and three SAT IIs. It also pays attention to international exams, so make sure you speak up about your A levels (they can also come in useful if you want to get out of required classes later on). There is also the option of an alumni interview – something that you should definitely take up (and remember it is as much for their benefit as it is for yours). Harvard grads love to talk about the best days of their lives in their dear old Alma Mater – and you can learn a lot about its good points (and its bad) by simply listening. So make the effort to jump through all the hoops Harvard puts in your path – in the long run, they're beneficial.

Finally, Harvard is one of the very few universities that offers FULL needs-blind financial aid to its international students. This is a wonderful resource and one that not enough people know about.

Your education here could, conceivably, cost you less than your tuition fees would in England. So definitely bear this in mind and, again, don't be ashamed or reluctant to enquire. American colleges are well aware of the huge financial burden they place upon their students and they are extremely clued in as to how to lighten it.

Famous Grads (more than a little hard to narrow down!)
John Adams, John Quincy Adams, FDR, Teddy Roosevelt and JFK – all presidents of this great nation
T. S. Eliot – biggest star in the Harvard poetic galaxy
Tommy Lee Jones – just to show we have our lighter side as well! (Roommate of Al Gore!)

Johns Hopkins

Baltimore, Maryland
www.jhu.edu
5,454 undergraduates, 13,139 graduates

How many students does it take to change a light bulb at JHU?
None – no one changes it. The less competition, the better.

For those students who like the idea of a small college with big research opportunities, Johns Hopkins is an option that should not be left off the list. This relatively small institution was founded in 1876 as the country's first research university and has gone from strength to strength since then. Situated in Baltimore, a city with dubious charms but only 45 minutes away from the nation's capital, Johns Hopkins has established a reputation for itself as a school based on hard work and success.

Johns Hopkins is most famous for its world-class medical school, and hypochondriacs should rest assured that any ailments contracted in this area will receive some of the best treatment in the States. While rivalry for the two undergraduate schools (one catering for the Arts and Sciences and the other for engineering) is less overwhelming than that at the med. school, both are considered to be excellent institutions. Situated on the Homewood campus in downtown Baltimore, these two relatively small colleges offer great facilities and unparalleled research opportunities. English, science and (unsurprisingly) pre-med courses have a reputation for excellence, as does the International Relations programme – a great option for Brits hoping to refine their diplomatic skills.

Each class at JHU is relatively small (around 900 kids) and fairly competitive, holding its students to a high standard. No matter what department in which you find yourself (and there is a great degree of flexibility), you will have to learn to argue logically and always be able to answer the many 'whys' thrown your way. This is not a school for fluffy thinking. Most of the professors are top researchers (a fact that, and you have been warned, can play havoc with their teaching skills) and expect their students to pay as much attention to fact as they do. The scientific spirit pervades the campus – even humanities majors have been known to moan about it! Perhaps because of this close connection between the sciences and the humanities, Johns Hopkins offers no core curriculum. As a result, many of the students double major or take minors between the two schools. No one here is afraid to work hard – and the university is more than happy to go on throwing degree options (including masters and doctoral programmes) at you!

Other grumbles about Johns Hopkins include the fact that its location is not all that it might be. While Baltimore is a big city, many of its entertainments lie quite some way away from the suburbs of campus. The Homewood neighbourhood offers the usual run of student attractions, but many JHUers feel the need for something more. And central Baltimore is, for those without a car, just that little bit too far. Luckily, downtown Baltimore and the Inner Harbour area have plentiful charms of their own and are closely connected by regular shuttle buses. Most students are quite happy with a social life based on campus parties, these nearby attractions and the occasional trip to Washington, DC.

Although the students love to complain, many actually admit they enjoy the small and friendly atmosphere of the campus. A fairly active Greek scene, numerous sporting events and such anticipated occasions as the Spring Fair keep everyone busy. And the fact that the freshmen and sophomores all live and eat on campus ensures a constantly vibrant environment. Juniors and seniors meanwhile benefit from having the option of living in off-campus apartments – something that is common in England but often impractical in America. JHU is a campus that is proud of its sporting prowess, affiliated with one of the top music schools (the Peabody Conservatory) and supports numerous extra-curricular activities. For those who like to be kept busy while enjoying a diverse and focused environment, this is a good place to keep as a 'potential' on that all-important short list.

Famous Grads
Michael Bloomberg – financial whiz and New York mayor
Madeleine Albright – political strongwoman!
Andre Watts - pianist

Massachusetts Institute of Technology (MIT)

Cambridge, Massachusetts
www.mit.edu
4,000 undergraduates, 6,000 graduates

How many students does it take to change a light bulb at MIT?
Five – one to design a nuclear-powered bulb that never needs changing, one to figure out how to power the rest of Boston using that nuked light bulb, two to install it and one to write the computer program that controls the wall switch.

Three little letters. MIT. So short and yet, along the same lines as those 'three little words – I love you', SO powerful. The Massachusetts Institute of Technology has a reputation and an influence in this world that cannot be underestimated. Some might think of Matt Damon frantically scrawling incomprehensible algebraic formulas in *Good Will Hunting*. Others may prefer to dwell on the fifty-six Nobel Prizes this college has raked in and the employment opportunities it affords. Whatever your association, for those of you interested in science (whether of the rocket or nuclear variety), this college, situated in the heart of New England, remains the best of the best.

The Campus
MIT prides itself in opening up to its students the mysterious beauty of the mind. It might have been in its better interests simultaneously to focus on the beauty of the campus. If your number one priority in picking a university is an aesthetically charming location, then MIT will sorely disappoint. As befits a college that focuses so much attention on the future, its architecture is modernistic and, for the most part, concrete. While it is not totally bereft of attractive buildings, it suffers badly by comparison with such 'quaint' neigh-

bours as Brown, Harvard and Amherst. This is particularly true in the seemingly eternal winter months where endless slush and snow enhance the general impression of overwhelming greyness.

All freshmen live on campus and, owing to the real estate prices in Cambridge, many upperclassmen opt to do the same. Campus housing is guaranteed for all four years. The eleven residential colleges and various fraternities and sororities provide the loci for student life and tend to be more charismatic and slightly more attractive than the rest of campus. Academia may take place in sterile classrooms off a succession of neon-lit corridors, but at least students return to a pseudo-home they have selected and made their own!

The ugliness of the MIT campus is fortunately relieved by the beauty of the surrounding area. While the campus is seemingly stripped of all vegetation, those in need of a landscape fix can find it on the banks of the Charles River. Cambridge, situated just across the river from Boston, is a bustling place that prides itself on being the most opinionated zip code in America. This is perhaps unsurprising given that the bustle is largely composed of throngs of students and academics from the illustrious, and ever so slightly pretentious, Harvard and MIT. Despite the opinions, all these whizzing brain cells make it a fun and lively town to hang out in.

The People
MIT is a campus obsessed by brains. If you do not relish the odd academic challenge and the daily competition that springs from being surrounded by America's brightest – this is not the place for you. MIT students are hard-working, ambitious and personally motivated. Walking through the corridors, you get the feeling that, not only does everyone know where they are going, they all plan to get there as soon as possible. Yet the fact that everyone on campus is extremely intelligent does not lead to excessive rivalry. Perhaps because many of these students were regarded as 'nerds' in high school, or because they all exist under the same stifling academic pressure, the majority of individuals are very tolerant of each other, resulting in a great sense of community.

As far as the ethnic composition of this community goes, MIT has one of the most diverse campuses of the great American colleges.

There is a particularly strong Asian community – making up about 30% of the campus – almost the same proportion as Caucasians. There is also a large international student presence (huge among graduate students). Those who do not salute the Stars and Stripes make up around 8% of each undergraduate class. MIT, evidencing its statistically obsessed mentality, reports that there are around forty undergraduate and sixty-five graduate students per year from the UK.

MIT has had some problems in straightening out the gender balance – science still being a testosterone-dominated playground! But MIT has none of the reactionary views of some English counterparts, and women can be assured of fair and enthusiastic treatment. Single women can get excited about the 58:42 ratio – although all applicants should bear in mind that a large percentage of students of both sexes rarely emerge from the classroom or library. MIT students frequently moan about the lack of attractive dating options on their campus – a half-fit girl or guy will swiftly become a hot commodity, but those of you who view university as the time of the fling may be disappointed.

For those who are prepared to leave the lab, MIT does offer and encourage a great deal of extra-curricular activities. While there are no nationally ranked sports teams, all students seeking a bit of fresh air can get their athletic fix through an intramural sports team (although PE also fills a part of the compulsory core requirements). Particularly popular, owing to the proximity of the Charles, are the delights of the crew team. Excess energy is also burnt off through music (very strong on campus), arts and social service groups. The dedication MIT students show to their test tubes is mirrored in other areas of their lives, and those anxious about whether activities exist outside the laboratory can breathe easy. The ethnic diversity of the campus also leads to a number of cultural activities. While most of these involve samosas or saris, there is a definite market for the Union Jack and tea at four!

The average MIT student has also proven time and time again that they are not without a sense of fun. Quite the opposite in fact. MIT is known for its brilliant pranks – they now have an entire museum devoted to their favourite 'hacks'. Students love to channel their brains into the absurd as well as the serious, and, given the size of their brains, the results are normally stupendous! One of the most renowned jokes involved rerouting an entire building's electrical system so the lights could be used to play a giant game of TETRIS. Other beauties have emerged from the long-standing feud with Harvard and include the disruption of several Harvard–Yale football games with various incendiary devices!

The excellence of MIT grads could not be attained without the excellence of their resources. This is a rich university, supported by both alumni and government funding, and almost all its students benefit. Whether through financial aid or the efficient and up-to-the-minute campus resources, the dollars that keep flowing into MIT help to make many a struggling student's time more comfortable. The fantastic computer system is, perhaps unsurprisingly, almost beyond compare, and the administration seeks to match its human efficiency to its mechanical one. Many MIT students, therefore, find that, while the academic pressure is on, the complexities of day-to-day living are much reduced.

Hitting the Books

Obviously, the concepts involved in splitting the atom and powering the world require a certain amount of brain and elbow work, and this is reflected in the MIT students' constant complaining about the vast quantities of work they are expected to do. This is not a place where you can expect to have the odd slack week (or even day). Still, the pressure is not as high as it has been in the past. Freshmen are all expected to follow a programme that covers certain basic requirements, but in recent years course grades now only appear on the transcripts as pass/fail. The rumour that this step was reputedly taken to reduce the number of freshman suicide attempts should give you some idea of the academic hothouse environment, but the action itself means that students can now relax a little as they strive to get their bearings.

MIT students may be perpetually busy, but at least they know they are getting the best possible instruction. As both a research and teaching institute, MIT is almost unparalleled. Both the professors and the teaching assistants who trawl through the guts of each class are extremely well-reputed. MIT students quickly come to appreciate that science's greatest discoveries come about through team work, and their subsequent relationships with both their peers and the faculty are extremely strong. There is a huge amount of back-up available.

MIT consists of five separate schools (Architecture and Planning, Engineering, Science, Management, Humanities, Arts and Social Sciences). Yet it is impossible to apply to a single one of them. All students at MIT must build on a similar academic base, and, by the end of their first year in college, the freshman class is well-grounded in the basic theories of a number of scientific fields. These initial classes are famed for introducing students to the fundamentals, often involving hands-on experience. Having learnt to crawl, students are then free to run wherever they choose. Nor does MIT restrict all its students to staring at a test tube. Majoring in the humanities is a possibility, and the fact that students can cross-register in an unlimited number of Harvard classes makes this a great opportunity.

Flexibility is the name of the game at MIT. Leaving aside the SCIENCE, SCIENCE, SCIENCE mentality, there is a great deal of choice. No major is declared until the end of freshman year, and, for the indecisive, further chopping and changing remains an option. Cross-registration between different departments is not only allowed but encouraged. Whether you are building roofs or investigating the neutrino, you will find a wide array of courses with class sizes varying from the large foundation courses to the most intimate seminars. Freshman year may see you confined to certain subjects, but after that the university (graduate courses included) is your

oyster. And the bureaucracy tries its hardest to make all the pearls as easily accessible as possible.

Those who believe that admission to MIT ensures they never have to write an essay, study a painting or learn a language again swiftly find they are mistaken. MIT undergrads face the same core requirements as other liberal arts colleges. Study abroad is popular for many (although perhaps not so applicable to the Brits who already are). There is also the option of combining the best of both worlds – namely the academic giants of Harvard and MIT. Despite the disdain in which these two giants hold each other, cross-registration between the two schools works wonders for both MIT poets and Harvard scientists.

No one denies that MIT academics are among the hardest in the world and the faculty gives its students plenty of chances to let off steam. One opportunity comes with the much anticipated, although still optional, IAP (Independent Activities Project) which takes place for four weeks each January. This stress-relieving period gives MIT students a chance to pursue whatever really interests them, whether social service, environmental research or further splitting of the atom, without worrying too much about grades. And all of this takes place with the full resources and faculty support of the university.

The intensity and rigour of the MIT academic system is renowned. If you are not prepared to work hard, you should not bother to apply (unless, of course, you are the reincarnation of Einstein in which case you shouldn't have too much trouble). Yet those of you who are reading this and cowering in fear should bear in mind that, while MIT expects a great deal from its students, it is fully and more than adequately prepared to offer them just as much in return.

Outside Those Ivory Walls

MIT may not be the most beautiful place in the world and it may not always be the most sociable. Yet for those in need of an aesthetic or party fix, there is one great advantage – the town across the river. Boston is THE student city – thronged with undergraduates from Harvard, BU, Tufts, BC and, of course, MIT. This bustling and fun student presence is only one part of the vibrant city. In architectural and historical terms this place is as near to London as you are likely to find on the US side of the Atlantic, and there is almost as much to do. And, for those on the marriage market, it supposedly boasts the greatest number of affluent singles in America!

From the clubs that throng Lansdowne Street (hired out regularly for student parties) to the Italian pastries that make the North End the place to eat, Boston offers something for everyone. MIT is lucky enough to be able to maintain its own campus while offering students all that the big city has to give. Whether you want to ice-skate on Boston Common, do a spot of shopping on Newbury Street or just laze on the banks of the Charles, Boston can provide it. And it's all just ten minutes away by the T – a one dollar subway system that would make Ken Livingstone weep with envy.

Boston is SO close that almost everyone ventures in there on a fairly regular basis. For those homebodies who are reluctant to step off campus, there are other options. Cambridge is a suburb defined by two of the greatest universities in America – Harvard and MIT. As such it offers a plethora of restaurants, bars and coffee shops. The best idea is to head for somewhere with 'Square' in the title – whether Harvard, Davis or Porter. For those whose wanderlust extends beyond good ole Massachusetts, there are also many travel opportunities. In the winter, good skiing is only a car drive away – the more adventurous can make it to Canada (with its lower drinking age) for the weekend. Another popular draw is New York, only a couple of hours away by train, or the infamous Chinatown bus – an inexpensive but bone-shattering ride!

Social Life

When one thinks MIT, one does not think party school. Images of working late by the glare of the library lamp are far more prevalent than visions of keg stands, sorority girls and police break-ups. While it is true that MIT is not going to break any records for its social status, it is unfair to suggest that people who go there do not know how to have fun. There may be large contingents who choose not to go out, but there are enough people who do to ensure all but the most hardened party animal a thriving social life.

The secret to social success seems to lie with the refusal to allow the work pressure to get to you. A couple of hours off will not, after all, kill you. Cambridge provides a multitude of escape options – bars, coffee shops and restaurants. And, if it lacks anything, it is a safe bet that Boston will have it in duplicate! If you choose to go to MIT it is important to make the effort to get out there and meet people. While the importance of the first few weeks has been slightly relieved by the recent decision to stop allotting housing after a roommate selection period, it is still vital to look outside the mountains of work and embrace the people who will help you get through it.

One way of finding a ready-made group of friends is by joining a fraternity or sorority. Unusually, for a New England school, these societies play a large part in the MIT social life, owning some of the nicer houses on campus and throwing some of the wilder parties. They are certainly an appealing option for many. Even Harvard students, who like to pride themselves on having a better social life than the 'scientists', have been known to turn up at and even enjoy the odd MIT party. This combination of frats, local options, extracurricular activities and the diversity of the student body ensures that there is a social life out there for every kind of MIT student.

Getting In

Difficult does not even come close to the application requirements needed for MIT. Impossible would perhaps be closer to the mark. There is a reason that this school has produced so many Nobel Prize winners – it takes only those students that it perceives to be, if not perfect, then as close as possible. Out of the roughly 10,500 applicants for each freshman class, only 1,500 are accepted (16%). When you consider that over a third of those eager seniors scored a perfect 800 on at least one of their SATs, you may realize what you are up against!

It is a given at MIT that you will be academically superior to 99% of the world. The ability to pull As out of nowhere will impress no one. Instead, the MIT admissions office likes to concentrate on signs that you know how to channel your immense brainpower. You need to show originality, initiative and an ability to stand out from the crowd. Wowing them with the fact you got top marks in your A level physics module is simply not enough. Prove that you have been noticed as well! America is full of science fairs and national academic competitions for its most prestigious students. If you came first in a British equivalent, tell them about it. If you have spent six months of your gap year doing a rocket science internship, don't leave it off that application. Once you have hit upon these indications of your drive and brilliance, you only need the glowing recommendations and brilliant grades and you're all set!

Remember also that most important of the ten commandments of application forms – show them you're a person. This is especially vital at a place like MIT, which many (especially those at liberal arts colleges!) actually believe is inhabited by mad scientists intent on producing robotic genii students. In fact, the MIT admissions board want to accept people who are not only notable for their scientific ability. If you play an instrument, speak umpteen languages or have a social conscience, you should make sure they know about it.

One of the best ways of doing this is through the interview. This part of the process is optional, but highly recommended, and a great way to find out more about the university. It is conducted by a member of the MIT Educational Council – a highly formalized name for the many grads of the university! Several of these alumni are scattered throughout the UK and it is easy to set up a meeting. These interviews, while intimidating, should not be scary and do not possess the power to decide on your admission chances, although they can certainly sway them. As long as you have spent a little time in preparing some serious (and light-hearted) questions and answers, you should be fine.

MIT is one of the few schools with a great financial aid programme for international students. If you need fiscal support to deal with the astronomical American fees, this is definitely a good place to apply. Consider this early though – financial aid applications need to be submitted in plenty of time.

Famous Grads
Kofi Annan – managing the UN is a breeze after rocket science
I. M. Pei – *the* architect of recent years
Buzz Aldrin – the second man to walk on the moon!

Northwestern

Evanston, Illinois
www.northwestern.edu
7,500 undergraduates, 6,000 graduates

How many students does it take to change a light bulb at Northwestern?
Two – One to screw it in and one to tell him how to do it according to the manual.

From Old England to New England ... For many Brits this leap across the Atlantic is quite far enough. Yet, for those adventurous souls seeking to leave the familial nest even further behind, there are a multitude of university options available outside the puritanical East Coast. One of the best of these is Northwestern University, an increasingly well-reputed college situated right next to Chicago. Best for those among you who wish to write, sing, doctor or act your way through university, it combines a strong academic reputation with a vibrant student body. Offering a chance to rediscover the secrets of the Midwest, Northwestern has plenty to give to those with that old pioneering spirit.

The Campus
Northwestern does not do things by halves. It has not one campus, but two; not one undergraduate school, but six. This plethora of opportunities might seem daunting to some, but in reality all its facilities are very closely linked. The main campus, inhabited by the six undergraduate schools and the grad school, is situated in Evanston, the suburb just north of Chicago. Founded in 1851, Northwestern is a pretty place. While it lacks the picture-perfect quaintness of some of the East Coast schools and the fierce modernity of other newer colleges, it succeeds in combining the old and

the new in a pleasing mixture – most important for any place in which you plan to spend four years of your life.

But the stunning thing about the Northwestern campus is not its architecture. Nor is it even the view, on fine days, of the imposing Chicago skyline. Instead, it is the great Lake Michigan which cuts right through the campus. This huge sea-like body of water, complete with beaches, is an integral part of Northwestern's charm. Whether you are of the ardent jogger variety or the more relaxed (aka lazy) BBQer, the lake will play a vital role in your college experience and offers the perfect place to go and vent your frustrations or homesickness.

Water, pretty buildings, lots of greenery and beautiful views combine with the proximity of Chicago, easily accessible by the 'el' train, to give you pretty much everything you could desire in a campus. But be warned. Those ER addicts among you will have seen the bitter wind and snows that pile up in Chicago. This is not just a TV effect. Winter in the Midwest is a killer, and the winds coming straight from the lake do not exactly improve the temperature. Sun worshippers, you have been warned.

The Northwesterner

The Midwest is a strange, strange place, and, for the average Brit, the first weeks at Northwestern may well be a cultural muddle. A large majority of Northwestern attendees hail from the Midwest – and will be AMERICAN, AMERICAN, AMERICAN in a way never dreamed of back in London. Their national identity will be far more pronounced than that of students at the reserved East Coast or hippy West Coast schools. In fact, in many ways those who attend Northwestern will gain a perspective on the society of the United States that the majority of Brits either never reach or simply fly over.

This is not to say that all Northwestern students are country 'hicks' or Mafia-esque Chicago transplants. In fact the majority of them are upper-middle-class conservatives. There is some racial diversity, with a large number of Asian students, but it is not as heterogeneous an institution as it might be (although, in comparison with the majority of British schools and towns, the UK student will probably find it a hot-bed of ethnic and religious persuasions). Nor does Northwestern have a particularly large international community – only 4% of the university hails from outside the States – so, if your goal is to surround yourself with a buffer zone of similarly confused Europeans, you may have a hard time.

Residential life at Northwestern is all-important in securing a good group of friends. This is partly due to the large size of both campus and college – factors that can make forging relationships difficult. Around 4,000 students live on campus, 2,500 either at home (all those Chicago residents) or off-campus, and a further 1,000 (no freshmen allowed) in sorority or fraternity systems. As a freshman you are guaranteed on-campus housing as long as you remember to request it in your application. Do REMEMBER or you could well find yourself left out in the cold! There are also eleven residential colleges at Northwestern, grouped around specific interests or skills. Some people choose to live in these, and there is an international one available. Be warned, however. Choosing to distance yourself from Americans is not the swiftest way to make friends. It is much better to throw yourself into the crowd from the beginning.

Northwestern students are known for being dedicated to a host of extra-curricular activities. Owing to the presence of the journalism, music and communications schools, the standard of publications and performances on campus is extremely high. The radio station is the largest student-run one of the nation, and the Waa-Mu theatrical show is nationally acclaimed. In this flurry of activity it pays to be an individual who likes to get involved. Of course, there is always the option of lying back by the lake and watching the world go by, but, if this is your entire life, then the frantic bustling of the average Northwesterner might eventually lead you to throw yourself in. Motivation, motivation, motivation – an essential quality of most Northwestern students and something you will need yourself if you plan to attend.

This is not to say that students here don't know how to relax or to have a good time. It's just that, everything they do, they like to do well. For instance, take a look at their football team, the Wildcats, a name you will be chanting in your sleep by the time you graduate. The Wildcats are not just a football team. They are also proud members of the prestigious Big Ten group. Football fever runs high on campus – one more example of an area in which Northwestern succeeds.

Northwestern is lucky in having a graduate school, research institutes and alumni that keep its finances fairly healthy. As a result, it has great resources, very modern sporting facilities and constantly renovated buildings. The general idea is that the sizeable endowment goes into making life easier for its students – something that is accomplished by an efficient and motivated college administration.

Hitting the Books (or newspaper, or sparkplug, or cello)
Northwestern is both made and crippled by the fact that it is not one undergrad university, but six. All six of these schools enjoy a good reputation, and their location on the same campus means that, as far as social and collegiate interaction goes, they are as one. The largest of them all, enrolling over half of each class, is the Weinburg College of Arts and Sciences – the typical American educational experience. Then there are the satellite schools, the School of Communication, the School of Education and Social Policy and the McCormick School of Engineering and Applied Science. Finally, there are two extremely good and prestigious colleges for those who have already found their vocations – the Medill School of Journalism and the School of Music.

On the surface, the presence of so diverse a collection of faculties seems great. Students can cross-register in courses between the colleges (although this can be a difficult process), and there are also opportunities for joint degrees. If you are the next Brunel or Bach and you want to study in a specialized environment that also contains students with many different interests, then Northwestern may well be the perfect place for you. However, if you remain unsure as to your vocation, you may find it both frustrating and difficult to bridge the gap between all these institutions.

Whichever college you end up at, and WCAS is an ideal choice for many of the great undecided, the words 'liberal arts education' are guaranteed to haunt your academic career. All six of the schools require that you take a series of core classes to round out your education. This in part soothes the frustration of those who want to combine classes from all the colleges. The engineers still end up speaking French and the musicians practising physics – in short, the great 'diversity' of subjects that all American universities pride themselves on is present in full force.

The average Northwestern student will also work pretty hard. This is a competitive college and the majority of classmates were at the top of their high schools. Professors push their classes to the limit but are normally available to those students who need a helping hand. The size of classes varies, but the larger classes (as at most of these schools) are broken up for more in-depth discussion groups. Students' lives are also made easier by the fact that it is now possible to do absolutely everything – from registering for classes to checking in with all professors – online.

One of the reasons that academic pressure is felt more at Northwestern is because of the trimester system upon which it operates. Actually, for the average British student used to the ritual of Michaelmas, Easter and Summer terms this is not a new thing. Yet it does mean the extra chore of having to take exams three times a year (as opposed to twice). This causes its own problems – terms are shorter and you have little time to get your teeth into one subject before you are handed an exam paper and told to go and register for another. For those who feel the pressure of exams, Northwestern, with twelve sets in four years, might not be the ideal location.

One of the great advantages of a Northwestern education is the importance that it places on exposing its students to the rough and tumble of the real work place. Perhaps because of its close ties to specialized areas (engineering, journalism, music), there are a plethora of internships and work experience options available. Students at the Medill School of Journalism actually have to be interns as part of their academic requirements. This commitment on the part of Northwestern to set you up for life beyond college is exemplary and an extremely important part of your college experience there.

Social Life

Northwestern is a fun university – a quality helped by its great campus and closeness to Chicago. The campus itself provides a wide variety of events, parties and entertainments for its students. The fact that so many are involved in theatrical productions, musical concerts and other artistic ventures means there is always something to do or see. Yet the housing system, the fairly large student body and the size of the campus can initially make it difficult to meet people and forge friendships.

The option of the fraternity or sorority is one method of meeting many people instantaneously and it has become huge on campus. This uniquely American concept is automatically the first association that 90% of Brits have with American schools. Not helped by films such as *Animal House, Legally Blonde* and the *Skulls*, most English students now believe that all Americans feel a compelling need to be part of something with an inexplicable Greek name, a bunch of really weird traditions and an eternal brother/sisterhood of similar freaks. In fact, this is not true. As Greek life at North-western shows, many simply see these societies as a way of expanding their friendship groups.

Greek life at Northwestern is very important. It is estimated that around 40% of the student body belongs to a sorority or frat, and 'rush' (the system of recruitment) takes place every fall. Many students choose to live in these societies and they are key in organizing many of the events and parties on campus. A recent attempt has been made to clean up their big-drinking, hard-living reputations, but alcohol still plays a large part in their lives. Some of the frats and sororities are socially based, others on ethnicities or interests. While those not involved often complain that Greek life is too dominant on campus, even they admit that there is not the fierce segregation between the initiated and the non-initiated that plagues other Greek-based colleges.

Outside Those Ivory Walls

'My kind of town, Chicago is' warbled Frank Sinatra. After four years at Northwestern you may well feel the same way. Chicago, the third biggest city in the United States, is quite unlike anything you will experience in the United Kingdom and offers a cultural awakening all of its own. Northwestern is ideally situated just north of the metropolis and only a short ride away by the famous 'el' train. Even when confined on campus, Chicago's skyline still dominates the view and, as soon as students have exhausted the good but few restaurants of Evanston, they can hit the town for a varied and fun night out.

It seems a waste of time to list everything that Chicago can provide in the way of amusement. Just as with London or New York, it is a veritable mixture of everything the student heart could desire. Plays, films, concerts and exhibitions appeal to the more artistically minded, while the sports teams, restaurants and clubs draw the red-blooded student crowd. And all of this takes place among some of the most magnificent modern architecture in the world.

Many Northwestern students only make the trip into Chicago on the weekends. Still others find that the campus provides sufficient amusements to prevent them from going in at all. Whatever your own opinion, it is a great place to have close at hand. The only possible disadvantage (aside from the weather!) is that Chicago does rather stand alone, isolated from both East and West Coast, and is that little bit further (culturally and geographically) from the motherland. Still, for a city that has everything you could possibly need, this factor soon ceases to be so important.

Getting In

Northwestern is on the up. As a result, so is the competition involved in getting in. A strong application and good grades are essential if you are to stand a chance. Out of the 15,000 or so applicants each year, only around 2,000 are admitted – a statistic very similar to the Ivy League schools. Although a similar standard is expected across all six undergraduate schools, students should be aware that you apply to the one that catches your interest individually.

The university requires all applicants to take the SAT I and the expected score is rarely below 1300. They also recommend SAT IIs. While 'recommend' sounds encouragingly as though they are actually providing you with the option, it is in fact HIGHLY advisable that you do take the exams. Rest assured though, Northwestern does understand, and take into account, the concepts of A levels. It advises anyone with predictions below a C to think twice before applying. Remember to put down your predictions, AS and GCSE results on your application form – they are a very important (and well-respected) guide to just how clever you are! Also bear in mind that if you are a young Mozart and aiming for the extremely competitive and excellent music school, an audition will be required.

Northwestern is known for its extremely tricky and abstract essay questions. Rather than the clichéd contemplation of 'my most moving moment' or 'my hero', required by most universities, these personal essays stretch the creative and imaginative powers of each candidate to the limit. Think before you write.

There is an Early Decision programme at Northwestern. Yet you should beware: unlike most other colleges, this university does not tend to forward applicants to the Regular Decision pile. If you plan to jump in early, you should really have your heart set on this being the only place for you. As with all these universities, it is important that your application gives a picture of you the person, as well as you the brain. After all, a sense of humour is one of the requirements listed on the application website!

There is no financial aid of any kind available for international students unless they are also registered as permanent residents of the United States.

Famous Grads
Cindy Crawford – if only all the girls looked like her
Warren Beatty – if only all the guys looked like him!
Charlton Heston – this place is heavy on future Hollywood stars

NYU

New York, New York
www.nyu.edu
18,628 undergraduates, 18,522 graduates

How many students does it take to change a light bulb at NYU?
Two – one to get the light bulb, one to go to the departmental adviser and see what the adviser thinks is best.

If you are the type of budding intellectual who believes that dressing in black, sipping espresso and reading Kafka in the corner of a dark, smoky coffee house is the way to go, NYU should be near the top of your potential US college list. Situated in the artsy Greenwich Village, near the ever-cool Washington Square, NYU draws in a diverse and talented bunch of students from across the nation and gives them a first-rate education in one of the most exciting cities in the world.

In recent years, NYU has turned itself around and gone from being a college that always played second-best to Columbia to being a college that is respected in its own right. Founded in 1831, for the purpose of ensuring that leadership and talent were fostered among all classes of society, NYU has had a chequered past. Even the campus attained no real coherence until recent years when students no longer had to commute all over Manhattan to get to class. Now, however, with a solid geographical location that provides students with a place to both live and work, the school spirit of the Violets(!) is growing stronger than ever.

Students who attend NYU tend to hold strong opinions and have specific interests. The University consists of several different undergraduate schools, many of which are world-renowned for their strength in a particular field. Among these are both the Tisch

Institute of the Arts and the Lawrence N. Stern School of Business. If you do not have your heart set on Broadway or Wall St, you can also find a place for yourself at the College of Arts and Sciences. The NYU community brings all of these disparate talents together and allows students to take classes between the schools. This flexibility enhances both your academic experience – you can be a history major and take sculpting – and, more importantly, your friendship groups, allowing thespians to mingle with economists.

NYU is noted for its tolerant and accepting attitude towards people of every kind of geographical, racial and ideological background. Some complain there is a liberal bias, but, while student debates are vigorous and common, they tend to take place in a good-humoured atmosphere. Certainly, no one seems to be bad-mouthing the institution. NYU applications have grown substantially over the last few years and there are now fifteen applicants for every place available.

For many students the most attractive part of NYU is its location. Few university students have thousands of restaurants to choose from, world-class art galleries to peruse, Central Park to go jogging in and the shops of Fifth Avenue just a few blocks away. Some complain that being in the city means that students find less time to bond with each other, and it is true that the campus and its inhabitants tend to merge with the surrounding city. But most students love this sense of being a part of the real world and getting to know people who live outside the bubble of academia.

This is not to say that NYU students do not take their studies seriously. In fact, the opposite is true. Approximately 60% of NYU students go on to further studies, and intellectual discussion is very much the ethos that binds the community together. While the academic programmes at NYU are fairly flexible, all undergraduates in the College of Arts and Sciences face the rigours of the Morse Academic Plan (the core curriculum devised by Samuel Morse of Morse code fame). This plan ensures that freshmen and sophomores have grounding in a foreign language, the arts, the social and natural sciences and other cultures. This rigorous programme prepares students for the intensive studies of their junior and senior years. NYU is academically excellent but can be very tough, and the emphasis put on the interests of the individual means that the individual has to do an awful lot of work.

NYU may not be the best college for you if you are the kind of person who likes to slack off or if you want a bona fide American campus experience. New York can be a lonely and scary place for those who are not gregarious or determined enough to go out there and make something of it. But if you have a city-loving side, a genuine interest in knowledge and an appreciation of faculty and students who feel the same way, then NYU is a good place to consider.

Oberlin

Oberlin, Ohio
www.oberlin.edu
2,800 undergraduates, 20 graduates

How many students does it take to change a light bulb at Oberlin? Three – one to change it and two to figure out how to get high off the old one.

Oberlin is the sort of college that either represents your idea of seventh heaven or hell on earth. Situated in small-town Ohio, about 45 minutes away from Cleveland, it draws an eclectic collection of students from all over America. The Oberlin student body is known for being progressively liberal, extremely politically correct and just that little bit wacky. Students tend to be experimental, eccentric and decidedly left-of-centre and the faculty members aren't much different. Proponents of the traditional Oxbridge or New England system will regard Oberlin as a radical's joke, but few would deny the strength of its academic reputation or the prominent position of many of its alumni.

Since its foundation in 1833, Oberlin has led the pack in liberal mentality. Kept together by abolitionist money in the early years, it was the first college to allow women and one of the primary educators of African-Americans. Oberlin students are, almost without exception, idealistic, and campus dialogue is defined by conversations about just how each and every individual can make the world that little bit better. Even deciding what type of milk you want to put on your cereal (organic? soy? goat?) can turn into a philosophical debate. Some might find this enthusiasm (which undoubtedly has a particularly American flavour) irritating, but most would agree that it is never boring.

While Oberlin prides itself on its diversity, it does attract a lot of well-off, white kids (often rebelling against parental authority), and a group of extremely talented musicians (studying at the world-famous Oberlin Conservatory). It also has a sizeable number of international students – around 7% of the fairly small class. Despite the disparate ideological convictions of most of the students, everyone tends to get along well – in part because of the confining nature of the attractive campus. Although Cleveland is only a short drive away, there is always something going on in Oberlin itself – a town that really functions as an extension of the eccentric student-body and offers just about everything they could want.

With a student body this motivated, there are any number of clubs, protests, papers and bands to get involved in, and it is a rare Oberlin student who does not seize every chance to participate. Academics are embarked on with the same enthusiasm, and student–faculty bonds are extremely strong. This is a university that positively encourages interdisciplinary learning, and courses are taken in a huge variety of subjects. Students are also actively involved in the educational process, whether they are giving their views to the administration or teaching a class in the Experimental College. Classes are small and challenging and known for being academically excellent. The well-reputed faculty caters for people who love to learn but who also love to discuss and dispute as they do it.

Students at Oberlin have a number of accommodation options that reflect the tolerant attitude of the campus. Oberlin offers nine programme houses where students can pursue a particular interest or belief. It also offers more standard dormitory situations as well as the famous co-op system where students live together and take on the responsibility of feeding and cleaning for themselves (something that sounds standard for us Brits, but is much less usual over here). The flexibility of the living system means that students can find out which of the many groups on campus makes them most comfortable without committing four years to any one of them.

The majority of students at Oberlin are extremely happy with their situation and love the outspoken and politicized atmosphere on campus. This is truly a place where rock musicians mix with classical violinists (again, the Conservatory is a focal point of campus life), poets with politicians and radicals with even more radicals. If you are a reactionary who loves George Bush and disapproves of sex, drugs and rock and roll (all integral parts of the Oberlin education), then this is not the place for you. But if you like to think outside the box and want a strong academic environment that permits you to learn with hundreds of like-minded people, then this may be one of the best options out there.

Princeton

Princeton, New Jersey
www.princeton.edu
4,600 undergraduates, 2,000 graduates

How many students does it take to change a light bulb at Princeton? Two – one to mix the martinis and one to call the electrician.

Think of every Ivy League stereotype your fevered mind can come up with. The beautiful buildings, the beautiful weather, the beautiful people strolling around in beautiful clothes and making beautiful conversation. Now take away the weather and you have a pretty good picture of how Princeton is generally perceived. This college is in many ways the most Ivy of the Ivies, a school steeped in East Coast tradition and catering to the most elite, and often most privileged, students America has to offer. Academically, it is a wonderful choice, competing with Harvard at the top of the rankings and in possession of some of the best professors on that side of the Atlantic. So, if you can deal with wearing an awful lot of orange for the rest of your life, then this internationally acclaimed university may well be a good choice for you.

The Campus
Princeton University was founded in the then small settlement of Princeton in rural New Jersey. The initial charter was given in 1746, making it the fourth oldest college in America. Today the beautiful garden state that was New Jersey is more frequently associated with petrol stations and strip malls and Princeton itself has embraced suburbia, numbering 30,000 inhabitants. Yet the Princeton campus, despite new additions both architecturally and among the student body (think, not just rich, white men), has remained relatively unchanged.

Princeton occupies a 500-acre spot in the middle of the surrounding town. This large area is filled with the traditional smattering of Gothic libraries, modern architecture and red brick houses. However, Princeton has succeeded where other colleges have failed, and all the buildings blend into one pleasant whole. Whether students are lounging on Cannon Green, rushing frantically into the famous Firestone Library or crowding out onto Prospect Avenue (aka the Street), they are almost always surrounded by beautiful architecture and a pleasant open space. Many of the buildings have played a historically important role in American history. The famous Nassau Hall (which also figures in the rousing Princeton song) housed British soldiers during the American Revolution and (after our somewhat ignominious defeat) served as the temporary capital of America under George Washington.

Small wonder that many students are only too happy to live in such a historical setting. It is expected at Princeton that all first and second years will live on campus in one of the five residential colleges. This division of these two classes into blocks of around 500 makes for a great community and a fun living experience in which you can very much make your own way while still having people around you who know the ropes. And these colleges have their own dining halls – delaying the pressure of choosing an eating club until your junior year. Juniors and seniors live in other on-campus dormitories (or, if they choose to, off-campus). They have the option of eating in the clubs on the Street or in the other facilities that the university provides for those who baulk at the idea of having to join a club to eat.

The Princetonian

For years Princeton gloried in the fact that the confines of its campus housed the offspring of the richest and most blue-blooded American families. It was truly the place where the WASPs (White Anglo-Saxon Protestants) went en route from Philips Andover and before they took their place in daddy's firm. Although Princeton eventually bowed to the times and opened itself up to an ethnically and economically diverse student body, hints of this privileged past linger on. It is generally assumed that the average Princetonian dresses entirely from Abercrombie & Fitch and that the whole campus swarms with similarly khaki clad, polo-shirted individuals. And it is certainly true that the undergraduates are among some of the wealthiest per capita in America. Although its preppy image may have lost ground in recent years, Princeton remains a fairly homogenous school and is resolutely conservative – refreshingly so for those British students who cannot stomach American political correctness.

This is not to say that Princeton admissions have not embraced the American plea for diversity. Over a quarter of the student body are, in fact, minority students, and 9% of the undergraduate population is international. The WASPy image may well stem from the fact that these students tend to form large and prominent cliques. It may also be true that four years at Princeton is enough to put even the most radical rebel in touch with his East Coast side. Yet, despite this aspect of the student body, it would be unfair to state that Princeton is intolerant of those different from this stereotype. As a whole, it is an accepting and friendly community with a strong school spirit ('Go Tigers') that houses students with a real love of the place they all chose to apply to. The huge amount of money that pours in from almost all alumni testifies to this very real devotion to the Princeton establishment (as well as to the consoling fact that Princeton grads do actually make money and you will not be a struggling student forever!).

There is one thing that links all Princeton students, regardless of race or finances: their brainpower. You will be amazed by the diversity of the people you meet, but you will be still more amazed by the things they have done and the things they say. This intelligence is coupled with a serious desire to achieve everything possible in a four year space. America is a nation of overachievers and Princeton is no exception. Whether playing in the orchestra, directing and producing your own musical, writing for *The Daily Princetonian* or joining the oldest debating society in America, you will find that your schedule quickly contains more hours for extra-curriculars than it does for sleep. And slackers among you should be warned, the University really encourages students to get involved with whatever interests them outside the library.

There is always something going on at Princeton and students never get the chance to complain that they're bored. Despite its Ivy

League (for which read all brains, no brawn) status, Princeton has a number of successful sports teams. And, if you're not out there playing, you're expected to be on the sidelines cheering and, if the mood takes you, painted like a tiger. It is impossible to graduate from Princeton without gaining a certain amount of the all-pervasive school spirit. Whether they are celebrating the beginning of their student lives with Opening Exercises or the conclusion with Class Day festivities, Princetonians do it with pride and a certain amount of rowdy singing. And, after all, what's not to be proud of?

Hitting the Books

There are only a handful of things you can criticize Princeton for – its paltry off-campus options and WASPy cliques being two of the most obvious. But there is one thing that only the very brave or very stupid dare to critique – its academics. It is undeniable that Princeton offers one of the best educations in America. The undergraduate experience is all the better because the university has a small graduate population and thus focuses its attention on the academics and well-being of the undergraduate above all else (in fact, there are no graduate programmes without an undergrad counterpart). This means that, during your four years of education, you will be spoiled for choice and continually under the attention of some of the best professors in both the nation and the world.

The commitment of the faculty is one of the nicest traits about Princeton. In recent years the university has gathered the best minds in America to teach its undergraduates (often luring them away from other top universities with substantial pay packages and tenure track offers). Today the faculty–student ratio stands at about 7:1, and all teachers are required to perform teaching duties as well as their own work. This means that students will actually end up being taught by the expert in a particular field as opposed to a struggling graduate student who speaks very little English. This access to such superb academic instruction can be one of the most challenging things about Princeton, but it is also one of the most rewarding. Princeton definitely expects commitment from its students, and the magnificent Firestone Library, which has more than 70 miles of shelving, is continually filled with undergrads exhausted by the pursuit of knowledge. Traditionally, students take four courses each semester until their senior year when they reduce their course load to three in order to focus on their thesis. However, many ambitious Princeton minds choose to take on even more. Princetonians are required to choose their major by the end of their sophomore year. There is a wide range of options, but some of the favourites include History, Economics, English and Politics.

Princeton also puts its undergrads through their paces in a core curriculum that, as at other universities, requires a certain breadth of knowledge. Some of this is instilled in the tradition of preceptorials, established by Woodrow Wilson and an integral part of the academic experience. These preceptorials place small groups of undergrads in weekly contact with their professors, providing them with a valuable opportunity to rub shoulders with the greats. Princeton rightly places a great deal of emphasis on this professorial–student bond and likes to talk about the importance and trust of this relationship. This is exemplified in the Princeton honour system. Once they sign a pledge of honesty, students are allowed to take exams without the presence of a proctor. This is symptomatic of the Princetonian attitude. They treat you like an honourable academic contemporary and you are expected to behave like one.

This emphasis on intellectual integrity is also put to the test by the hoops that Princeton requires you to jump through in your junior and senior year. Unlike most universities, Princeton insists that all its undergraduates write both a Junior Paper (the JP) and a senior thesis. Although this is a significant amount of work, Princeton believes that it helps you to organize yourself for the real world as well as, after you recover from the numerous sleepless nights and caffeine fixes, giving you a real sense of achievement. Throughout the process you are under the guidance of a member of the faculty, another example of the care that the Princetonian administration takes of that most lowly academic individual – the undergraduate.

Be warned, however. Many students complain that the care Princeton takes of its undergraduate can, at times, be overwhelming. The core curriculum is extremely rigid and students often feel their academic flexibility is limited. Study abroad is also not really encouraged by the administration — although many justly feel that the calibre of academics on campus means that they have everything they want right there.

Social Life

It is easy to imagine the social life of the average Princetonian fifty years ago – lots of white men sitting around in their eating clubs, sipping port, smoking cigars and talking about the next crew race against Harvard. Times have changed since then, and the increased diversity in the student body has shaken up the stuffy traditions of previous generations. Princeton students now find every weekend on campus offers a vast variety of plays, musical performances and cultural occasions, not to mention the odd celebration of a football triumph or two. Whether your taste is for drunken keg stands and Blink 182 or a quiet espresso while you listen to Brahms, you will find like-minded individuals on the Princeton campus.

One thing has, however, remained relatively unchanged despite the passing of the years. The process of selecting and then participating in an eating club is still a unique part of the Princeton experience. The twelve eating clubs situated on the Street provide the nutritional and social haven for juniors and seniors. The clubs cater for around 150 people and, until fairly recently, if you wanted to eat you had to join. Nowadays the clubs are optional, but many students still view them as an integral part of student life. Some of them are open to all through a lottery process while others maintain the old exclusivity, selecting their lucky members in the 'bicker' held at the end of sophomore year. These clubs are far more than just a munching-ground. Given Princeton's lamentable lack of off-campus options, they also serve as party centres for the university and frequently provide anyone who wants it with a drunken Saturday night. (It is also widely rumoured that one of them has a cache of A grade papers available for its members to use when writer's block strikes!)

It should be noted that, while Princeton has a great on-campus social life (helped by the genuine efforts of the faculty to build a student centre that actually has fun stuff going on), it remains exactly that, on campus. Some students are fine with staying in the same square mile every weekend of their college career, but others find it quickly becomes insular. Luckily for these people, NYC is only a short trip away.

Outside Those Ivory Walls

Princeton has many things going for it, but the local town is really not one of them. Princeton, New Jersey is an old and established place, and has notably failed to embrace the twenty-first century. As a result, students frequently complain they have very little to do once they step off campus grounds. The area is charming, with small restaurants and pretty houses, but there are none of the bustling bars, clubs and shopping districts that characterize university life. Even student eateries are limited in number, most of the restaurants falling into either the expensive-bring-the-parents or gross-who-would-eat-that categories. English girls will, however, be relieved to know that there is a Laura Ashley on site for all your smocked frock needs (something that makes you wonder about the Princetonian woman's dress sense).

Luckily, however, most Princeton students are satisfied by the active social life on campus supplemented by the basic fare of cinema, meals and coffee in local Princeton. And, when they feel the need to kick up their heels and have some metropolitan fun, New York and Philadelphia are only an hour away by frequent train and bus services. This is short enough to make a day trip feasible and a weekend trip extremely enjoyable. However, most students simply cannot be bothered to make the effort.

Finally, if you go to Princeton you should also not forget about the natural world outside the campus walls. Although 'beautiful' New Jersey is sadly no longer beautiful, it does have areas that are extremely special, and it is definitely worth while devoting at least one weekend of your undergraduate experience to exploring this bit of America (strip malls optional).

Getting In

Nobody ever said it was easy. Princeton is almost always near the top of any ranking lists you choose to look at, competing normally with Harvard (but always slightly behind!) for that valuable first place. And since the university made an effort to open up their doors to people other than Mr My-great-great-great-grandparents-sailed-on-the-Mayflower, admissions have become even more competitive. The university estimates that it can only accept about 11% of those who apply, and, given that there are almost 15,000 applications, this makes for an awful lot of disappointed people.

Princeton requires that all applicants take the SAT I and three

SAT IIs by the December of the year in which they apply. These results are then submitted with the form itself – a tasteful production with lots of orange. The Princeton form is one of the longer of the college applications, consisting of questions as varied as 'What's your favourite cereal?' (you have to wonder if they are running psychological assessments on your answers), as well as the more typical 'What has changed your life? How do you deal with X?' questions. The last section provides a glimpse into Princeton's old admissions process, asking you to state any relatives who trod the New Jersey ground before you.

Interviews with alumni are also available and should be taken up if possible as they provide you with a good opportunity to discover more about the place you are considering devoting four years of your life to. Princeton expresses a particular interest in special talents and your life outside your books. So, if you have built an orphanage in Afghanistan or sung in Westminster Abbey, shout out about it. Americans are not a modest nation, and British reticence, especially on application forms, will do you little good.

Princeton offers an Early Decision programme for those set on their choice of college and eager to forge ahead. If you want to take a gap year, you must apply, be accepted and then defer. However, Princeton does actually encourage this British idea (something that is not true of all US colleges). Princeton also does offer financial aid to international students – another rarity in the States and something that is well worth considering. Make sure you consider it early, however, applying for this (especially from an international status) takes a while.

Famous Grads

Woodrow Wilson – President of the United States
Ralph Nader – most hated politico of the moment
David Duchovny – smart in real life as well

Stanford

Stanford, California
www.stanford.edu
6,600 undergraduates, 8,000 graduates

How many students does it take to change a light bulb at Stanford?
One, dude.

There are many contenders for the crown of best Californian university. The dazzlingly smart CalTech puts in one bid that cannot be lightly dismissed and both UCLA and UC Berkeley are strong runners. But time and time again the victory goes to a school that is widely judged to be one of the best universities in America: Stanford. Situated in Silicon Valley, 30 miles from San Francisco and commanding views of the Golden Gate Bridge, Stanford is an institution that calls out to students and academics all over the world.

The college was founded in 1891 with the death of millionaire Leland Stanford's teenage son. Devastated by the loss of his only child, he and his wife decided to build a university that would enable them to treat the children of California as their own. Over a century later, their legacy has developed into one of the greatest of the American colleges – a highly selective and incredibly successful academic institution that (provided you can deal with the trek to California) should be at the top of any prospective student's list.

The Campus
This 'Ivy of the West Coast', does not only rest on the laurels of academic success, it also enjoys one of the prettiest campuses around.

As with all the Californian schools, the year-round sunshine and blue skies do much to increase the atmosphere, but even in the event of a freak Ice Age, Stanford would remain a beautiful place. Initially the Stanfords used the land as a horse farm and the old Red

Barn still stands today. Now, however, a spacious and well-planned campus surrounds it. While planning their college, the Stanfords consulted with the deans of several prestigious universities and their efforts more than paid off. The famous Frederick Law Olmstead (the driving force behind New York's Central Park) was placed in charge of the design and the campus remains an architectural and aesthetic success 100 years on.

Stanford is connected to the nearby town of Palo Alto (smack in Silicon Valley) by a mile-long drive lined with palm trees. As you walk down it, the attractive sandstone buildings of the main campus open out before you. The Main Quad, with its Californian-style architecture is the heart of the university – the home of the beautiful Memorial Church (complete with mosaic front) and also the site of the infamous Stanford 'Full Moon on the Quad'. In one of the more fun college traditions, incoming Stanford freshmen experience a rite of passage when they are kissed by outgoing seniors on the Quad under the first full moon of their first year (definitely a custom that many a desperate senior across America wishes their college would adopt).

Other notable parts of the campus include the Herbert Hoover observation tower (named after Stanford grad and US president) which offers fantastic views of the local area, the bustling White Plaza and the amazing Rodin collection (the biggest anywhere in the world except his museum in Paris). Stanford campus, despite the somewhat frightening threat of the next big earthquake, is one of the most beautiful on offer and any student who gets to spend four years lounging around on the sun-soaked quads gazing out at the rolling foothills (Stanford-owned, of course) will hardly be able to believe their luck. Rainy old England will seem a long way away.

With such a beautiful location on offer it is hardly surprising that around 94% of students choose to live on campus for all their time at university (especially when one considers the cost of off-campus living). Stanford has really solved the issue of options in housing, and students have the choice as to with whom and how they want to live. Students can live in dorms that span across the four years or within their year group – most specifically in the freshman houses that give nervous first-years a chance to find their feet among their peers. Others can choose to live in dorms that are themed to their liking; some explore a particular ethnic aspect of the States (such as the Native American culture), while others focus on a particular interest. Whatever your choice, chances are that you will find living on 'The Farm' (the cognoscenti's name for the campus) to be an incredible experience. Affection for Leland and Jane Stanford's contribution remains strong – their family crypt becomes the site for the annual Halloween celebration where students show their thanks by literally dancing on the graves of the founders.

The Stanford Student

The Stanford motto, chosen by Mr Stanford himself, is 'Let the wind of freedom blow'. As far as freedom of personal choice among the student body of Stanford goes, the wind seems to be blowing pretty hard. Although this is a much smaller (and thus much more personal) body of students than its UC neighbours, the diversity among each class is still extremely high. Stanford has always had a reputation for catering to a particular type of student – in one sense the Californian equivalent of the WASP – in other words the privileged legacy child in a West Coast setting. Yet while such individuals play out their fathers, lives on the Stanford campus, the admissions board ensures that classmates from a variety of ethnic, religious and socio-economic backgrounds dilute them.

Despite this diversity, many feel that the campus is dominated by Asians and Californians. Europeans may find they are less well-represented here than at East Coast universities – Stanford seems to attract many of the Asian international contingent (it is after all closer to home!). Other students complain this uneven balance makes the university cliquey and that friendships are forged on the grounds of race or bank balance rather than values and interests. However, this is a grumble that holds true for many universities and Stanford does no worse than anywhere else at dealing with problems that continue to plague a polycultural America.

Most Stanford students quickly find their place in the community and are constantly amazed by the wealth of experience that their classmates bring with them. School spirit runs high and the laid-back attitude of Californian life permeates the campus. Many state that while things seem quiet on the surface, students are working incredibly hard in order to stay afloat. Yet, while it is undeniable that

Stanford students face a large amount of work, the sunshine and the beautiful campus add to an atmosphere of relaxation that snowed-in and built-up New England schools can never achieve. Whether they are cheering on their home football team (the Cardinals) in the Big Game against Berkeley, or releasing their exam tension in the cathartic Primal Scream (which ripples across campus in the build-up to finals), Stanford students tend to be a united and high-spirited bunch.

The Stanford sports teams are internationally renowned. In the Sydney Olympics, Stanford athletes won more gold medals than all but fifteen countries, and their teams regularly dominate the West Coast rankings. The importance of athletics on campus does mean that there is a strong jock culture – something that can be off-putting for the average, lazy Brit who may find that going to the gym swiftly becomes part of his day.

There are masses of other activities to get involved in at Stanford, and many are willing to sacrifice valuable relaxation time for a higher cause. A large percentage of students are involved in outreach programmes in the surrounding area, while others hone their journalistic skills at the *Stanford Daily*. If you prefer to spend your spare time in a more relaxed setting (and provided you have some musical talent), you can always join the university band whose spirit-raising pranks and much-loved mascot (The Tree) add extra cheer during football matches and other school events. Cheerleading is big as well – now may well be the time to achieve that Bring It On moment (and boys, don't worry, there are spots for you!). Whatever your interests, you will find that someone else shares them, the only thing that may be hard to find are the hours in the day to pursue them.

Hitting the Books

The reputation that Stanford has upheld for so long does not come easily. No matter how relaxed their attitude, every student will tell you that being enrolled at Stanford means that hard work is expected and that slacking off now only means longer hours at a later date. Leland Jr (the teenage son in whose memory the college was conceived) was an extremely precocious child – speaking languages fluently and amassing a large collection of art by the time of his death aged fifteen. Stanford students live up to his illustrious memory by putting in long hours and asking a lot of questions. Many even take co-terminal degrees – a special Stanford programme that allows you to earn your bachelors and your masters in one fell swoop.

Stanford students are, however, helped in their pursuit of knowledge by a brilliant faculty. Getting an offer of tenure at Stanford is a mark of distinction in the professorial field and many academics flock there for the scholarship and the sunshine. As a result, Stanford has one of the strongest faculties around and a student-teacher ratio of 7:1. Professors are very approachable but this is not a cosy hand-holding institution. While the relatively small size of the campus means that teachers are much more available, the level of academic competition means that no one is going to be standing over you and watching your every move. Getting that reading done is up to you, but you can be assured that if you do work your way through *War and Peace*, or the finer elements of molecular science, some of the world authorities will be on site and more than willing to discuss it with you

The easy relationship that exists between pupil and teacher at Stanford is aided by the trust that has been built up over the years. Stanford students adhere to an Honor Code, requested by the students and indicative of their serious approach towards their studies. These studies encompass a core curriculum which requires courses in writing, language, the humanities, natural sciences and foreign cultures. This firm liberal arts foundation is intended to act as a springboard for the more intensive work required once you have finally selected a major. And, owing to the three quarter (rather than semester) system, under which Stanford operates, students are able to sample more classes in less time before they sign up for a particular department. Again the faculty are on hand to help you every step of the way, and the flexibility (no major has to be declared for the first two years) means that you have a huge amount of time to make up your mind. And, if you need to take time off and go abroad, the university is behind that too – in fact Brits can take advantage of an exchange programme with Oxford.

Stanford has always been a progressive school, offering co-education from the time of its founding and demanding that its students be not only cultured but also useful. Today it continues to advise students on how they can best serve the world at the same time as furthering their own knowledge. Many students go on to public service careers or join the Peace Corps, although an equal number succumb to the lures of Silicon Valley (almost everyone at Stanford finds themselves in a computer science class at some point), and the somewhat more fiscally rewarding task of serving technology. In a sense this is simply giving back to the university – much of Stanford's wealth stems from Microsoft and Hewlett Packard.

Social Life

Stanford students tend to be an outgoing bunch and their relaxed attitude to life makes this a fun school to attend. Even for those students who come from out-of-state, the Californian approach becomes contagious and the weekends are a time for lying back and enjoying oneself (however many deadlines one has). Californian clean living is also catching and this is not a campus that has a big interest in drugs, hard partying and the seedier parts of a rock-and-roll lifestyle. It is, on the other hand, a campus that (in a nice liberal Californian way) takes a fairly lenient approach to alcohol. For those English people who fade away without a local pub as a gathering ground, this is one of the few American universities that might not cause too many withdrawal symptoms. Having said that, drinking to excess (very unhealthy) is not a regular feature of campus life, except for at the Big Game against UC Berkeley when, frankly, anything goes.

Much of the social life at Stanford revolves around the dorms and people spend a lot of time simply hanging out, visiting the 24 hr pizzeria or catching the weekly flicks the university puts on. For those who fancy a more rowdy party, the fraternities and sororities (to which around 20% of the campus belong) tend to spring into life at the weekend when they often open up their doors to the whole campus. If you are the type of individual who needs more than a few keg stands, some guitars and a lot of chatting, then San Francisco offers a wealth of opportunities – although getting there and back takes a large chunk out of your Saturday night.

Rival schools like to say that '99% of Californians are hot, 1% go to Stanford'. This assessment is more than a little cruel and Stanford attracts its fair share of beautiful people. Few people actually complain that Stanford itself does not offer sufficient social life.

Whether they are attending Homecoming, fighting over tickets for the annual Viennese Ball or kissing as many people as possible in moonlit Quad, Stanford students know how to have a good time (and those who don't swiftly learn how to take advantage of the local area).

Outside Those Ivory Walls

A Stanford student is never short of things to do, places to go or people to see. While the actual town of Stanford is not much used by students, there are hundreds of weekend options available in the wider area. The nearby Palo Alto, famed for its amazing shopping, is often dismissed by students as too expensive and not particularly nice but San Francisco, the city of the Golden Gate Bridge and every cosmopolitan excitement imaginable, is less than an hour away by the much-used Cal Train. San Fran is a wonderfully diverse and cultural city with mind-blowing views, great shops and delicious restaurants for those who get bored of the already numerous collection situated closer to home. Once a year a huge scavenger hunt in the big city is organized in an attempt to familiarize freshmen with the local area – and many find themselves going back on a much more regular basis. The trip to the big city winds its way through Silicon Valley – the technological heartland of America, a place populated by Stanford grads and one of the most prosperous regions of the States.

For those who would rather leave big cities and industrial genius behind them, Stanford is also near to a wide array of more rural pursuits. The Sierra Nevada mountains, with their numerous hiking options are only four hours way, the Pacific is a relatively short drive (45 mins) and the ever-popular Death Valley experience can also be done in a weekend. The famous Yosemite National Park is also easy to get to, and many students choose to camp there when life at home is simply getting too much for them. Californians are obsessed with healthy living and environmental awareness. Stanford is unusual in managing to combine the two with a location that offers every technological and big-city benefit. Whether you are into raving, windsurfing or just lying around in the quad chatting to friends, you can be sure that Stanford will cater for your every taste.

Getting In

Unsurprisingly a university as good as Stanford is highly selective in its admissions process and extremely competitive to get into. In recent years approximately 12% of applicants have been admitted – and these are the ones with the strongest grades and highest recommendations. As around half of the students hail from California (thus honouring Leland and Jane Stanford's original intention), there is an additional pressure on international students and those from the forty-nine other American states. Stanford, however, has always been proud to educate those from across the world and international applications are very much encouraged. A certain amount of financial aid is also a possibility, although it does not operate on a needs-blind process, and thus requesting it may well jeopardize your chances of admission.

Stanford (like almost all other US schools) likes to say that it places a huge amount of importance on the personal achievements of each prospective student. While a large part of this may just be college-speak, it is still important to emphasize on your application all you have achieved outside the classroom. The Stanford student body is a diverse and dynamic group of people and you need to prove yourself worthy of entry into this elite club.

Stanford does not offer interviews – believing that they are entirely subjective and offer no real insight into a person's character. It is thus important that you make your personality appeal on paper – as there is no chance of selling yourself in person. Both Early and Regular Decision options are available – although Early Decision is binding so be sure that you really do want this to be your first choice. As far as tests go, Stanford requires the SAT I and three SAT IIs, one of which must be writing and the other of which must be the Maths 2C (bad news for those who quit maths at the first opportunity!). When the new SAT Reasoning begins, the SAT II writing will no longer be mandatory.

Famous Grads

William Hewlett and David Packard – Stanford did a good job admitting these guys
John Steinbeck – one of the stars of a long literary tradition
Sigourney Weaver – an educated actress(!)

Tufts

Medford, Massachusetts
www.tufts.edu
4,700 undergraduates, 3,000 graduates

How many students does it take to change a light bulb at Tufts?
Two – one to change the bulb and one to explain how they did it
every bit as well as any Ivy Leaguer.

Ask anyone to expand on Tufts' reputation and they will probably
mention two things - elephants and international relations. This
small but prominent university is dominated by its college mascot
(who appears in statues all over the campus) and its excellent international relations programme (most famously at the graduate
Fletcher School of Law and Diplomacy). Tufts has long been known
as the school that steals from the waiting-lists of the Ivy Leagues, and
recent action on the part of the past two presidents has seen it
progress in leaps and bounds. Particularly welcoming to international students (probably because we give the Americans a chance
to practise their diplomacy skills outside the classroom), it is a good
option for those looking at small and well-reputed New England colleges.

Tufts is situated just outside Boston (easily reachable by a short
walk and the fabulous T). The campus is located on a hill and is
divided into new buildings and older, more classical architecture.
Students like to say that they get the best of both worlds – the benefits of the nearby thriving city and the aesthetic and spatial advantages of being slightly apart from it. Certainly the campus is both
spacious and pretty and the hill provides you with plenty of sledding
opportunities (and a constant work-out). Some of the college buildings are more than a little shabby (the administration recently has
started to pour money into renovating them), but the whole is both

attractive and easy to get around. Approximately 70% of students live on campus and freshmen and sophomores are required to do so. After that students can choose from on-campus options, fraternities and sororities or local off-campus housing.

The student body at Tufts hails mainly from the northeast and tends to fall into the preppy, New England, middle-to-upper-income tier bracket. While its international relations programme does attract students from across America, this is not the type of school that will introduce you to a huge variety of students. Reputed (a little unfairly) as a second-tier Ivy, Tufts brings together ambitious and hard-working students who are eager to get involved in everything. Despite the notably hard freshmen requirements, Tufts students pursue multiple extra-curriculars from day one. The college daily and weekly newspapers (unusual in a school of this size) are particularly well thought of and the campus is strong in both communications and media. And if you're the singing type, the numerous a cappella groups are also well-known.

Tufts is also highly thought of for its strong academics. Despite its size, it has a good research programme and its students can pick from a huge number of courses. Not only can they cross-register in classes at many other Boston schools (if they cannot find something in the extensive course catalogue), but the more culturally minded ones can also pursue joint degrees at the New England Conservatory and the MFA. And out of the thirty-four credits you must fulfil, only ten of them need be in your major. Students have a great deal of flexibility in choosing their interests and over a quarter of them pursue a double major. This does not mean, however, they are exempted from all requirements. Tufts ensures that its students receive a well-rounded education and its freshmen can frequently be heard moaning about all the courses they have to take. However, throughout this process, the heavy involvement of the professors enables undergrads to get the best possible advice whenever they need it – the thing that has really earned Tufts the reputation it enjoys today.

Tufts has also managed to maintain a strong school spirit outside the classroom. If you are an ardent football fan, this is the place for you. Both soccer and baseball dominate the campus and pull out many a cheering fan to their respective fields. And if sports aren't your thing, the university also regularly invites world-renowned speakers to address its students. As far as your social life goes, the local area has some great restaurants and Boston offers pretty much everything you could need. Freshmen on campus tend to be very involved in the Greek system (of which around 15% of undergrads are members), but the older years prefer to look elsewhere for weekend amusement. And would-be dating addicts should beware. Many students complain that Tufts lacks any romantic scene – most of your classmates will either end up in long-term relationships with each other or stick to those partners from out of town.

If you are interested in applying to Tufts, you must submit a common application (sparing you much of the individual hassle that other schools impose). It is recommended that you take SATs in the subjects you are likely to be interested in (as well as, of course, the obligatory SAT Reasoning). Alumni interviews are available and a good idea. Financial aid is, however, unlikely to be an option – Tufts has only limited funds available for its international students.

University of Michigan

Ann Arbor, Michigan
www.umich.edu
24,472 undergraduates, 14,500 graduates

How many students does it take to change a light bulb at UMichigan?
Ten – one to change the bulb and nine to act as the Supreme Court to affirm the decision.

Brits who are really looking to get away from the *Brideshead Revisited* Oxbridge experience, and who believe that East Coast America is simply not far enough, would do well to consider the University of Michigan. You may not even know where Michigan is (think mid-West, lots of lakes), but this top public university has a reputation for being one of the best of its kind. With an excellent faculty, highly rated research facilities and a campus that numbers some 25,000 undergrads and 14,000 graduate students, UMichigan is the place to go for those who want a great education in very different surroundings.

The huge size of the student body can be one of the most off-putting things about UMichigan. It is all too easy to become just one more face in a crowd and the shy and retiring type will find the sheer throngs of people just too much to handle. The mass of undergraduates means that class sizes (especially on the introductory level) tend to be larger than usual and students need to pick their courses with care if they are to interact with professors on a personal level. For those who have the drive to do this, however, the benefits are many. UMichigan is a buzzing place, with hundreds of options and a real student atmosphere. Although there may be none of the hand-holding that is common at smaller liberal arts colleges, the average Wolverine (as they are known) develops an independent spirit and an ability to pursue what he or she wants.

UMichigan is one of the best public universities in the USA (competing with UVA and UCLA for the title of most prestigious). As such it has severe restrictions on who it can admit. Over two-thirds of the Wolverine student body are from the state of Michigan itself. The average Brit may feel more than a little lost among all these mid-Westerners, but there can be no doubt that it will be a formative cultural experience (and that accent is sure to come in handy in striking up conversations!) Meanwhile the magnitude of the campus means that over 6,000 of the undergrads are from out of state (a number that makes up many a small East Coast college) – a fact that offers the international students (who comprise 4% of the student body) plenty more diversity.

Although many Wolverines may feel that they are one among many, few of them complain of feeling alienated from their school. UMichigan has some of the strongest school spirit on offer in the US. As a proud member of the Big Ten (a group of the sporting elite), a passion for sports dominates the Michigan campus and footballers (many of whom turn professional) are treated as gods. If sports aren't your thing, the diverse interests of the campus ensure there are plenty of other options on offer – including programmes at the nationally renowned School of Music, an active theatre community or high-class journalism at the *Michigan Daily*. And if all this simply sounds like too much work, opportunities for leisure also abound. UMichigan is situated right next to the great Michigan

Lakes (which make the English Channel seem like a mere puddle) – an environment that is perfect for sailing, water-sports, hiking or simply (on those rare sunny days) sunbathing.

UMichigan's reputation is also made by the town in which it is situated. The lively and student-dominated Ann Arbor has become a byword for college party, referred to by students as A^2. While almost all freshmen live in the on-campus residential dorms (offering a great initial bonding experience), the upperclassmen (sophomores, juniors and seniors) migrate to the many available off-campus apartments. This off-campus living is unusual in the US and provides students with a great opportunity to experience real-world living while still benefiting from the student lifestyle. Ann Arbor is a great place to do that. Equipped with all the coffee shops, restaurants, bars, and general hanging-out spots that a student could need, it saves UMichigan from being just another big school in the middle of nowhere. And for those who really feel the need for some big-city living, Detroit (home to Eminem and not the most sophisticated place in the world) is just 45 minutes away, while Chicago is four hours by the reliable Amtrak train.

UMichigan is not just a school renowned for its social life (which, with its combination of frats, sports and environment is undeniably good) or even for its sporting prowess. It is also famed for providing its students with a truly good education and offering them academic and research opportunities that many schools with an even stronger reputation cannot provide. Prospective students apply to one of the six undergraduate schools – most of you would be looking at the College of Literature, Science and the Arts (more commonly known as LSA) although engineering, nursing, art and design, kinesiology(!) and music are also options. Once students are admitted they can take courses across the six schools, choose from a wide variety of majors ranging from jazz studies to astronomy and even invent their own should nothing that's on offer appeal.

UMichigan has a huge and dedicated faculty offering a vast number of courses – in everything from birdwatching to the history of St Petersburg. Undergraduates find themselves facing a number of requirements designed to give them a solid grounding in such basics as maths, writing and a foreign language. Small seminars (some of them open just to freshmen) also ensure that students don't get lost among the huge numbers and offer a chance for personal interaction with some of the leaders in their fields. Meanwhile themed semesters give students the chance really to focus on whatever offbeat topics the dean of the college has chosen for that term. Despite its size, this is a school that treats academics seriously and actively encourages you to follow your interests.

If all of this makes UMichigan sound like the place for you, then make sure you get all your application material together in good time. This is one of the few colleges that operates on a rolling admissions process (first come, first served) and applying early helps your chances significantly (as does your parents moving to Michigan). UMich remains a highly competitive school (especially for out-of-state students) so make sure your SAT scores and application essays are up to scratch and don't expect any help in the way of financial aid (no provision is really made for the international crew).

University of Virginia (aka UVA)

Charlottesville, Virginia
www.virginia.edu
12,700 undergraduates, 4,500 graduates

How many students does it take to change a light bulb at UVA? Thirteen – ten to form a student committee to vote on whether changing light bulbs is a violation of the Honor Code, one to change the bulb, one to hold the keg that he's standing on, and another to attribute electricity to Mr Jefferson.

Thomas Jefferson's gravestone is decorated with his three proudest achievements. The first two, the Declaration of Independence and the Statute of Virginia for Religious Freedom remain integral parts of the great American dream. The third, his foundation of the University of Virginia, is accessible not only to those who salute the Stars and Stripes but also to lowly Brits! The university – known to one and all as UVA – has possibly the most beautiful campus in the States, is situated in a sweet Southern town and offers an education that, despite its public status, is nationally acclaimed. This is a school for those of you looking for a truly American educational experience, based on the doctrines of one of America's truly great men.

The Campus
Beautiful does not come even close to describing the campus at UVA. Those of you with an aesthetic bent who believe that nothing in America can begin to rival the 'dreaming spires' of Oxbridge, should think again. All of Jefferson's architectural endeavours were impressive (as a day trip to his home in Monticello will prove) and UVA is no exception. Founded in 1819, the campus (or grounds as it is popularly known) has a classical feel with beautiful white buildings situated around vast expanses of green. Jefferson believed that

a university should be akin to an academic village – scholars and faculty coexisting in a community consisting of many splendid buildings.

The showpiece of the campus is the magnificent classical Rotunda, situated at one end of the hallowed Lawn and a worthy match for rivals such as the Bodleian Library or Trinity College, Cambridge. The Lawn itself, still boasting all of the original student residences, is the central part of the UVA campus. Living on the Lawn is a serious matter. Only the most popular and respected members of the faculty take up residence there. As for the students, living in one of these historical sites requires a whole new application process. A small group of individuals who are judged to be exemplary members of the UVA community are selected annually for the privilege of inhabiting this hallowed spot.

UVA has a large student body but its campus, still for the most part contained within the original boundaries, helps to provide a centre for the community. And beyond the confines of the university and the bustling town of Charlottesville, the Virginian countryside is among the most beautiful in the United States. Rife with tales of the Civil War, the rural areas are perfect for historians and nature-lovers while hikers can set off up the Blue Ridge Mountains and keep going for miles. AND, perhaps of most importance, in Virginia the weather smiles on you. This is one of the few places in America that actually has all four seasons (most manage three at best). This may not seem the key selling point for a college, but the joys of spring and autumn should not be underestimated!

The UVAer

UVA is – as it states – the University of VIRGINIA. Despite its national reputation, its focus (sharpened by the state-funding it receives) is on educating the inhabitants of the home-state. Just under 70% of the student body are locals taking advantage of the slightly easier admissions process and lower tuition. Such homogeneity will make your attendance at UVA very different from that at any other American college. You may, in fact, come home as a Virginian.

This transformation starts when, even as an international student, you are required to register as a Virginia Domicile. This is only the beginning. Those of you who thought the Civil War was over should think again. If you have not managed to glean from the British educational system what or when this nation-changing event was, prepare for a steep learning curve. Virginia was the epicentre of Civil War action – caught as it is between the North and South. As might be expected, UVA – with its local student body – has some decided views on the subject. Nor should you neglect the instrumental role that Jefferson played in throwing the British out of America – spawning jokes that you may become sick of in rather fewer than four years!

Leaving history out of the equation, the homogenous aspect of UVA can be somewhat trying. Although Jefferson dreamed of an international student body, admitting the first foreign student in 1826, the modern percentage of students from outside the States now only stands at four. And even though the admissions office is flooded with applications from out-of-state individuals, the emphasis is very much on the Virginian. UVA prides itself on having a large minority student body – some 23% of the whole. Yet students continue to complain that, in keeping with Southern history, there is a certain amount of segregation between black and white students and the university remains dominated by upper-middle-class white Southerners. As a Brit you will probably be a source of fascination, but you may also feel a little alienated.

Yet UVAers are united around certain aspects of the campus. UVA is a school steeped in age-old traditions that bring together even the most diverse members of its community. From its own language – this is perhaps the only college in America where you will be known as a first year rather than a freshman (making Brits feel right at home) – to such peculiar customs as scrawling graffiti on bridges or streaking across the Lawn, UVA will ensnare you in its web of customs. Regardless of ethnic, national or religious background you become a product of a very individual school, marching to the same beat and singing to the same rousing football songs as every other one of your peers.

As a student you have a variety of choices regarding your accommodation. The university, leaving aside the hallowed Lawn residences, is split between the old (McCormick) dorms and the new (Alderman) dorms. There are also a number of students living in the frats and sorority residences. Furthermore, there are residential colleges, including the recently opened International Residential College. While these may seem tempting it is, as always, recommended that you throw yourself into the 'Americanness' of things straight away. There is little point in crossing the Atlantic solely to surround yourself with your countrymen.

It is remarkably easy to become involved in the UVA community. This is a school where everyone likes to do everything. Societies of every possible description exist on campus and it would be tough to find nothing that captured your attention. And although some claim that student publications and radio stations are often overlooked, the reputation of the papers that do exist is very high. For the sporting kind (and be warned, sport at UVA, as all over America, is a huge part of one's daily existence), there are a multitude of intramural and varsity sports in which you can get involved. And, good news for the Brits, our experience in soccer and lacrosse won't go amiss. These are areas in which UVA excels (although cricket is sadly excluded!).

Hitting the Books

Honour. Honour. Honour. This uniquely Southern concept led to a culture that involved great romances, pistols at dawn and lifelong feuds and friendships. It also provided the background from which an integral part of the UVA experience was to emerge – the Honor Code. This system was designed to ensure co-operation and trust between faculty and students and was founded in 1842 following the fatal shooting of a professor by a pupil! While pistols no longer play such a vital role in academic dealings (to the relief of many unpopular faculty members), the Honor Code lives on.

'On my honor as a student I have neither given nor received aid on this exam/assignment.' During your four years at UVA this will become a mantra that will haunt your dreams. By signing your name to this trust agreement, you earn yourself the privilege of taking exams and tests without invigilation and in any situation you like. In return you neither cheat nor take advantage of the situation. The student-run Honor System also entitles you to local privileges – e.g. the writing of cheques in local shops. Such a simple code allows students a great deal of freedom and all UVAers are extraordinarily proud of this part of their heritage. Don't be tempted to cheat it.

Any violation of the Code results in expulsion. Harsh treatment, but necessary in preserving one of the most historical and moral aspects of UVA.

Perhaps due to the atmosphere of trust the Honor Code creates, the relationship between faculty members and students is great at UVA. Although it is a huge school, the class sizes are kept fairly small, many more intimate seminars are offered and professors are known for being extremely accessible to their students. There is the inevitable problem of grad students teaching classes, but the professor-student ratio remains at 15:1 and most make a real effort to get involved on campus. Again it was the sainted Jefferson who extolled the importance of the faculty–pupil relationship and, as you should all have realized by now, his every word became UVA law. UVA is officially divided into six undergraduate schools: Arts and Sciences (where in all likelihood you would head), Architecture, Engineering, Nursing, Commerce (very well-reputed), and Education. There are a huge variety of courses available and a great deal of flexibility in your selection. While the liberal arts requirements that underpin most of these American schools still exist at UVA, they are measured by hours rather than course matter and are a great deal shorter as a result. Twelve hours of maths and science in four years is really not that bad!

Even deciding on a major does not limit your options. A student has to complete 120 hours of credit to graduate and while requirements vary for different subjects, only a maximum of forty-three of these need to be in your chosen subject. Traditionally this is a great school for those interested in English and History, but the overall subject standard is very high and you would be hard pressed to find a subject here that didn't interest you. Students also benefit from the great resources (the library filled with — you've guessed it – Thomas Jefferson memorabilia) and a very efficient administration that does everything possible to make the rigours of student life easier.

You have to work hard to get into UVA and this trend continues once you have been accepted. The university takes pride in being known as 'the public Ivy' and its academic standards are often as high as those of its prestigious counterparts. Having said that, while the majority of students are pretty ambitious and push for these higher grades, it is possible for more slothful individuals to tread water for most of their academic careers. This discrepancy of standards is perhaps encouraged by the fact that the majority of UVA students are known to be less cut-throat than their Ivy League rivals. Perhaps it is because of the faculty presence and interest in undergrads, perhaps because of the Honor Code or perhaps because of the laid-back Southern atmosphere. Whatever the reason, UVA manages to balance academic pressure and active socializing without most students slipping into either nervous breakdowns or alcoholism!

Social Life

Those of you who worry that your social life may suffer as a result of attending university in a country that often seems to positively prohibit fun, need not fear. This fate will not await you at UVA – a school that parties as hard as it works. In fact this school offers you the best of the private and the public – the academic standard and status of the former and the party reputation of the latter. Even the most hard-working of UVA students can be torn away from their desks at the weekends and the more relaxed crowd party far more regularly.

Socializing comes in many forms at UVA. The town of Charlottesville offers one option – its bars and restaurants certainly help to warm up individuals for a fun night out. The campus itself has a plethora of social opportunities – from the ever-popular football games thronged by students clad in blue and orange to events organized by the 300+ societies on campus. The UVA administration also takes students' social lives into their own hands. As a campus steeped in tradition, there are several annual events to which everybody turns out.

This is a Southern school and as such is heavily influenced by the Greek scene. Fraternities and sororities thrive on campus – adding to the reputation of UVA as one of the best places to party. Around 30% of all men and women on campus are involved in these societies – opting to live in the houses situated on that social mecca: Rugby Road. The societies are very diverse and for the most part those who are not actually members do not seem to feel excluded. Far more isolated are the notorious Secret Societies that live on despite the scandal that surrounds them. Of these the most renowned is 'Seven'. The pranks are seen, the reputation lingers, but the members remain unknown – although when they die, the bell tolls seven times at 7 o'clock on the seventh day afterwards while the grave is covered with flowers in the shape of (you'll never guess) a seven. Definitely the stuff of which horror movies are made!

Outside Those Ivory Walls

If you hail from that species 'big-city dweller' who cannot walk on a street without traffic, whose lungs collapse if the air suddenly falls below the required pollution quota and who believes that Hyde Park is the country, then UVA will probably not be the university for you. Despite the beauty of the campus, and there would be few nicer places to feel isolated, this is not an urban university and cannot provide the facilities and entertainments of the big cities.

Charlottesville occasionally claims to be a city, but it maintains the feel of a charming and fun Southern town. It may not have the diversity of night clubs and bars that NYC and Boston offer, but it has good restaurants, thriving book and film festivals, cinemas, shops and a great student feel to it. Most well-known perhaps are the 'Fridays after Five' concerts given by bands at the end of each week. On other days most students head for 'the corner' – a collection of bars, coffee shops and restaurants close to the grounds. If you are wandering further afield, the university bus service helps to facilitate movement. Although nightlife may not be the strongest feature of the town, UVA students do not, for the most part, complain. A sociable bunch, they throw their own parties, make their own fun and see Charlottesville as a great springboard for their adventures.

The remarkable countryside outside UVA is also a great place to explore. Even those of you who shun the delights of throbbing blisters and wet canvas might be excited by the proximity of two nearby ski resorts. And if you're really feeling the need to escape, then Richmond is close enough – just find a friend with a car. The national capital (Washington DC) is also situated just two hours away by the omnipresent Greyhound bus service.

Getting In

This may be a public university, but the admissions requirements and process rival those of the top private schools. In a typical year around 14,000 students apply to UVA. Roughly 5,000 are accepted. This is about 40% – a fairly competitive environment, and much more so when you consider that 70% of them have to be from within state. Everything rests upon your application – there are no actual interviews for this university. As always, SAT Is are required. The bad news is that so are SAT IIs and not just in the subjects of your choice. As well as the standard writing exam, applicants are required to take the maths option and one other. All of these need to be done by the December of your final year at school. A high academic standard is regarded as crucial by the admissions mafia.

SAT scores at UVA generally fall in the 1300ish range. They should be backed up by strong personal essays on the admissions form – some shorter questions and the longer 'who are you really'-type challenge. It is hard to say what else helps you to get into UVA. There is a preference given to those from Virginia – but it may be difficult to get away with that pretence! As with most universities the children of alumnae are also considered somewhat special, so if you have that in your favour, be sure to mention it. There is a binding Early Decision option that it may be advisable to take if you know that UVA is the only place for you.

There is no financial aid for international students unless they are also permanent residents of the United States. There are, however, a handful (literally) of scholarships available which may be worth pursuing. Due to its public status, UVAs tuition is significantly less than private schools, but still ludicrously high in comparison with the English system (unless you manage to get your hands on one of those scholarships).

Famous Grads
Edgar Allen Poe – kooky Southern writer
Tina Fey – *Mean Girls* writer and SNL presenter
Ted Kennedy – JFK's brother and US senator

UPenn (and Wharton)

Philadelphia, PA
www.upenn.edu
9,900 undergraduates, 8,996 graduates

How many students does it take to change a light bulb at Penn?
Only one – but he gets six credits for it.

Benjamin Franklin was not a man who believed in the merits of
relaxation. Not content with setting up fire services, acting as international diplomat or inventing the stove, the lightning rod and bifo-
cal spectacles, he also found the time to found one of the top academic institutions in America: the University of Pennsylvania.
Today, this thriving campus set in lively Philadelphia continues to
churn out students in the Franklin mould – practical, business-
minded and dedicated to public service. But UPenn has come a
long way from those early Quaker roots. If you're looking for an Ivy
League education with a busy social life (that ever-elusive combination), then this could well be the place for you. And if you aim at
being the next fat cat on Wall Street, then the excellent undergraduate business programme at the Wharton School should be top of
your list.

The Campus

Founded in 1740, UPenn likes to lay claim to its status as the oldest
university (but not college) in the United States. Situated right next
to the Schuylkill River, a great location for the crew teams, the 260-
acre campus provides a nice, safe, green respite from the bustling
chaos of downtown Philadelphia (a mere 5 minutes away by bus).
The campus plays host to four undergraduate schools: the College
of Arts and Sciences (your most likely destination), the Wharton
School (money, money, money), Penn Engineering (for those keen

[177]

in following the founder's footsteps) and the School of Nursing (one of the best in America). Students from all of these schools live and work together on one campus along with thousands of graduate students.

Penn is a big school but the layout of the campus is easily negotiable and makes it feel smaller than it really is. Despite the age of the institution, the campus architecture does not come close to emulating the splendours of Oxford or Cambridge. Attractive stone buildings are positioned next to modern eyesores – chief among them the hideous, but extremely good, library. Not all the architecture is a disaster, however, and Penn students take pride in the fact that College Hall provided Charles Addams (alumnus) with his inspiration for the Gothic and ghastly Addams family mansion. Others love the fact that, despite the proximity of the big city, UPenn has really achieved a rural campus feel. Whether you are sunbathing next to the statue of Ben Franklin on the Green or throwing a frisbee in the attractive Quadrangle, there is a real feeling of a cohesive campus.

This sense of community certainly helps when nervous freshmen arrive at Penn as one among several thousand. Although it is easy to feel lost in the crowd, the freshmen residential halls swiftly dispel this feeling. Most Penn freshmen ask to live in the Quad – a good idea as it houses most of the youngest class and a great deal of parties! Sophomores, juniors and seniors have the option of living in less attractive high-rise residential buildings, their fraternities or off campus. Many choose the latter – congregating in local University City and colonizing areas around the bohemian South Street.

The UPenn Student

UPenn's mascot is the Quaker – a strange symbol for rousing school spirit at football games, but an appropriate representation of the school's tolerant and laid-back attitude. Partly because of its large size and partly because of the attempts of the university administration to encourage diversity (it was the first Ivy League to have a female President), Penn is a school that offers something for everyone. For the British student coming from fairly homogenous England, the levels of racial and ethnic diversity (around 40% of the student body are not white) may well be surprising. These myriad backgrounds and cultural perspectives make Penn what it is: a lively and tolerant place where everyone can find a spot that suits them. And, with 9% of the student body international, even the Brit can't feel too lost.

This diversity is not to say that Penn does not suffer from the stereotypes that sadly still define many academically elite institutions. 15% of the student body are legacy kids – some of whom can probably trace their ancestry back to the days of good ole Ben. And, while the WASPy contingent may be less at Penn than at Princeton or Harvard, many students complain about the huge number of JAPs (Jewish American Princesses) who descend upon the campus. The average Brit may not grumble about the presence of beautifully turned out, impeccably socially aware and filthy rich individuals that haunt Penn's grounds, dominate its social scene – and are only too keen to bond with Englishmen on the off-chance they might know Prince William. But for others, the appearance of so many wealthy NY socialites can be a bit of a turn-off. Luckily the size of the Penn student body is such that it is easy to lose those with whom you do not see eye to eye. But if you hold strong communist ideals or believe that fashion trends are the manifestation of the devil, then Penn may not be the place for you (turn to the Oberlin section now!)

Penn's student body is also ambitious and practically minded. While intellectualism undoubtedly has its place on campus, most people have more interest in business matters – a trend undoubtedly enhanced by the presence of the Wharton School kids. Students here are concerned with money and many of them, from both Wharton and the College, end up going through i-banking recruiting at the end of their senior year. This ambition leads to a strong work ethic and an intense curiosity about how the world actually works. Penn students are constantly involved in different activities, taking on different internships and asking questions to which they expect concrete answers. This work ethic and sense of activity infects the whole campus and whenever something is going on (which is all the time), you can expect it to be of the highest quality. Publications, like *The Daily Pennsylvanian*, theatre groups and social service programmes are all prominent parts of many students' daily lives.

This work ethic should not suggest that students do not know how to have fun. UPenn takes pride in its social success and offers a welcoming environment to new students. While competition may run high for the prized A in class, outside the academic sphere, people are relaxed and proud of their friendly community. Sports matches against their long-term rival, Princeton, draw huge crowds as do such quirky traditions as Hey Day when, at the end of the school year, juniors greet their senior year by donning straw hats and canes and marching through campus (possibly the most English experience you will see in a US university).

Hitting the Books

UPenn students may love a good party, but they are also known for working as hard as they play. And in a place renowned for its academic excellence and friendly faculty, such a decision is fairly easily made. Our friend Ben was a self-taught man who believed in the merits of a thorough liberal arts education as well as the ability to apply what one learns in college in the real world. Over the centuries, UPenn academia has evolved to honour both of these goals through an extensive curriculum and a plethora of classes.

Many of the stars of the academic solar system find a home at Penn and undergraduates may well find themselves in a class taught by the professor who really 'wrote the book' on the subject. Faculty members are required to teach undergrads and many of them willingly embrace the task. But while the faculty–student ratio is extremely low (at 6:1), many students complain that they find themselves in huge introductory classes where they are just one in a sea of faces. This may be true, but there is a simple solution to the problem. Americans are by nature a little more forward (some might say pushy) than their reserved British contemporaries. If you want to talk to your professor on a one-to-one basis, you have to make the effort to seek him out, go by his office hours and prepare yourself for an intelligent conversation. If you do this, you will soon find that your working relationship goes from one among many, to an actual intellectual bond.

It is true that many of the professors at Penn are also working on their own research and that graduate students take up much of their time. But the sheer numbers of classes offered to the undergrads, and the flexibility they enjoy in selecting them, means you can really shop around until you find the faculty member who most interests you. Students can take courses across the board and across all four of the undergraduate schools. Many of the financially savvy members of the college spend a lot of time taking economics classes at Wharton, while Whartonites find themselves heading back to the College for a dose of something that is not numerically inclined.

In fact, in its effort to make sure its students are well-rounded members of society, Penn insists on various core requirements. Students in the College will find themselves embracing the traditional tenets of the liberal arts education – including a stint of a foreign language, some maths and the humanities. Wharton undergrads who already find themselves taking finance, accounting, management and marketing, also face various liberal arts requirements as do their nursing contemporaries. This mixing up of different interests and academic strengths makes for a much more interesting classroom situation. And the fact that you don't have to choose your major until the end of your sophomore year means that if one of these required courses really grabs you – you may go from being an intellectual history buff to a Wall Street wannabe after all.

The one serious complaint that many undergrads have about the Penn system is its lack of advising capability. Because majors are decided upon so late, students are not assigned departmental advisors until well into their college careers. As a result students sometimes find they make the wrong choices without anyone saying anything about it. Some like the freedom this limited support network provides but others, especially those who would rather be lazy than put in the groundwork to make a successful schedule, find it difficult.

On the whole, however, Penn students find their academic environment stimulating and absorbing – a fact that sees many of them go onto grad schools following their BA. Those of you heading to the Wharton School should also be alerted that – should you turn out to be the fiscal whizz of your class – you may have the chance to get a Masters in Business with only one additional year of studying. This is a great and prestigious opportunity and if you're leading the pack in accountancy or economics, make sure you make enquiries about this possibility. Also, bear in mind that a degree from Wharton is the way to go if you know from the start that you want to concentrate on economics and don't want to have to fight your way into business school at a later date.

Social Life

If you asked the average Penn student what aspect of their school they are most proud of, they would probably give you some pretentious answer about Ben Franklin's legacy or the human capital available to them on campus. Secretly, however, they're thinking about how their party scene beats that of their Ivy League rivals into a small hole in the ground. Jealous Harvard and Dartmouth students might grouch about how Penn students never actually have to do any real work, but when it comes to college parties as the movies portray them, they are forced to admit that Penn stands alone.

Much of this social scene takes place on campus, although there are numerous options available in town for those who prefer upmarket restaurants and elite clubs. Penn itself hosts a number of fraternities and sororities whose parties attract people from all over campus. While joining these Greek institutions may seem a bridge too far to those British students who associate fraternities with cults and initiation with *Animal House* madness, these parties are normally open to all and do not necessarily require that you sign your life away to Delta Kappa Gamma. Unsurprisingly, these events attract huge numbers of socially eager freshmen – excited by the prospect of free beer (Quaker restrictions do not make evading the drinking age law in Philadelphia any easier) and drunken interaction with the opposite sex.

For those looking for a quieter life, the rowdiness of the frats is easily avoidable and the pattern of the next three years on campus settles into a quieter routine of dinner parties and smaller get-togethers. With such a large number of students around (even if we don,t count the graduates), the chances are high that you,ll find people to suit your pace of social life ˆ even if said social life simply consists of sipping English Breakfast and watching the world go by. One final word of warning, if you do decide to make the JAP contingent your friends ˆ they party hard and they party expensively. So be prepared and start expanding your wardrobe now!

Outside Those Ivory Walls

Nowadays the 'Streets of Philadelphia' look a great deal more cheerful than they did when Bruce Springsteen first moaned about them. This old Quaker city may have been through a rough time in the past, but it is now as vibrant and as safe as any of its East Coast contemporaries and is a great place to go to school. It also has the largest airport you have ever seen – perfect for flights back home (or to the Caribbean if you need a little weekend break when the snow has set in for the fifth time that week).

Students at Penn can never complain about being bored. Not only do they enjoy a fun campus social life, they are also a mere 15 minutes on foot away from all the delights of the big city. Philadelphia offers all the sport, arts, culture, nightlife and shopping that any undergrad could require and the majority of students take advantage of this. Penn gives you the chance of experiencing life in a thriving city, without the manic pace of New York Life or the dodging-bullets sensation of New Haven.

For those who seek a more outdoorsy experience, the vast Philadelphia park system provides ample room for rural pursuits, while the proximity of Penn to the station gives you the option of travelling to all the hiking grounds and leisure opportunities you could desire. For the city-minded, Amtrak is available to take you up to NY and Boston or down to Washington DC. And for those who love to shop, one of the biggest malls in the States is only a half-hour drive away. Philadelphia is one of the best-connected cities around, and it would be a short-sighted student who couldn't find anything to do there.

Getting In

Getting into Penn is no easy feat. Although a few years ago, the application numbers for the college dipped, recent statistics have shown it is now as competitive as ever. The school may be a large one, with proportionately more places, but it also draws proportionally more students. The admissions office estimate they accept around 20% of applicants. Unfortunately for international students, this number is somewhat lower. Many foreigners apply to Penn and it is estimated that only around 13% get in. As with all these traditionalist schools, it helps if Mummy or Daddy sported the Penn colours back in their day.

Penn's admissions requirements consist of an SAT I and three SAT IIs and a strong personal essay designed to reveal your true self to those making the decision. This is really the chance to show yourself off on paper – so don't let your British reticence hold you back, American students will be only too proud to boast about their Junior Nobel Prize or seven Olympic medals. A non-mandatory interview is also available and is a great chance to both sell yourself and find out more about whether Penn really is right for you. While some financial aid is available, international students do not share the needs-blind status of their American contemporaries and any requests need to be made well in advance and may easily not be granted.

Famous Grads

Donald Trump – shame it didn't teach him about taste
Charles Addams – a little twisted but very cool
Warren Buffet – he may have quit after two years but he's still doing pretty well

Vanderbilt

Nashville, Tennessee
www.vanderbilt.edu
6,300 undergraduates, 4,800 graduates

How many students does it take to change a light bulb at Vanderbilt?
Two - one to call the electrician and one to call daddy to pay the bill.

You may think you know America but until you have visited the
strange, strange land of the deep American South, you can never
call yourself a true aficionado. Although the Civil War has long since
been fought and won, the spirit of the South continues to loom larger than life. Plantation life may be over but the opinions, accents
and chivalry live on. Nowhere are these more apparent than at
Vanderbilt University in Tennessee. Situated a mere five minutes
from Nashville, the great music hot spot of the South, Vanderbilt is
home to Southern belles and gents in their present form. In fact, if
Scarlett O'Hara or Rhett Butler were searching for their ideal campus right now, the odds are that good ole Vandy would fit the bill
nicely. With a strong academic focus, a thriving Greek life and a
campus full of groomed and beautiful Southerners, Vanderbilt
offers both a good education and a unique American experience.

The Campus
Vanderbilt was founded in 1873 by Commodore Cornelius
Vanderbilt, a self-made millionaire who never actually visited the
place but did manage to provide it with both its good Dutch name
and its somewhat unusual mascot (the Commodore). The buildings
are set in parkland that was recently designated a national arbore-
tum and the campus defines southern elegance. The spacious 380
acres are marked by old brick buildings, green quads and countless

varieties of tree for shade on sunny Southern days (or shelter on the many rainy ones!). Places such as Alumni Lawn form the central focus of the campus and play host to student traditions such as the Rites of Spring – an outdoor party that embodies Stravinsky's pagan fantasies.

The pleasant surroundings and tight-knit community mean that most students choose to live in dorms or fraternities situated in the grounds themselves, allowing them easy access to all facets of student life at all times. In fact students have been known to refer to their campus as the Vanderbubble and are almost uniformly content to stick to the boundaries of what is, in fact, a relatively small university. Many of the lazier variety moan that if you don't have a car (a crucial part of existence in the South), Nashville, while only five minutes away, is just too much effort. Yet a little exploration beyond campus confines is well worth the additional exercise or cab fare. Nashville is prosperous and lively, the home of bluegrass music and extremely proud of its Southern heritage. It also offers Vandy students a wonderful alternative to the occasional monotony of campus life. Visiting musicians from all over the States have ensured a plethora of restaurants, bars and concerts that combine the highest of national standards with that little bit of genuine Southern flavour. For an English student whose previous experience of the South may well have been limited to drunken renditions of 'Cotton-Eyed Joe', the combination of Vanderbilt and Nashville will provide a sound cultural and academic education that would be hard to find elsewhere.

Southern Belles and Southern Balls

Some have compared the average female student at Vanderbilt to a debutante on the evening of her first ball - with one key difference - she is like that all the time. Certainly Southern culture, with its dictates on gentility and elegance, demands that both the Southern male and female are always immaculately groomed, well-mannered and charming. While the men who attend Vanderbilt certainly don't seem to be complaining, girls who have embraced the laddish behaviour of the twenty-first century often find it more than a little difficult to adjust to the strictures of such a life. Many grumble that it is considered a crime to appear in public at Vandy without a full face of make-up and the perfectly accessorized outfit. Others say that such an atmosphere condones snobbery and creates problems for students who like to express themselves in other ways. At the end of the day Vanderbilt requires a certain personality type – after all the reputation of being a member of the hottest campus around necessitates a certain amount of effort.

Ironically, the British student may feel more at ease in the rarefied environment of the 'old South' than many of their North American contemporaries. The code of manners that continues to subtly influence Vanderbilt life today is akin to that which still reigns in England. Southerners are an exceptionally friendly bunch but they have an initial reserve and social protocol that has vanished in the Northern States. English people may well find this easier to deal with, although they should be warned that this is a university with a long tradition of men asking women on formal dates to football games! While some will assuredly regard the atmosphere as verging on the cliquey and stuffy, others will find that this polite way of life makes for an enjoyable college experience. Vanderbilt is certainly one of those universities that students should visit before applying to.

Approximately half the students at Vanderbilt hail from the South and there is an international student body of around 8%. As an Englishman (or woman) you need not worry about being accepted into the ways of American culture. The United States as a whole has a strong Anglophilic tendency, but this is particularly marked in the South. Once you are past the initial accent barrier, you will find that you and your roommates will be trading vernacular gems for years to come! In fact you may well find it easier to fit in than many an American of a more diverse ethnic background. While Vanderbilt has made an effort to incorporate people of all backgrounds, many students note that it is a very homogenous environment.

Those who complain about the lack of diversity also bemoan the dominance of the Greek system within the Vanderbilt walls. In the best tradition of all Southern schools, Vanderbilt's social scene is largely dominated by the existence of sororities and fraternities. It is estimated that around 50% of women and 35% of men join one of these houses, often living with their sisters and brothers and confining their socializing to specific letters of the Greek alphabet. While this may all be a little too *Animal House* for your liking, it is undeniable that many of these frats throw the best parties on campus and are an integral part of the Vanderbilt existence. Clever students learn how to accommodate them while refraining from sacrificing themselves on the altars of rush week. After all, there are plenty of other options available to those who are willing to seek them out and Vanderbilt's reputation as a school that knows how to have a good time was never built solely upon the members of Sigma Chi.

Academics

Honourable behaviour extends from the dating game to the classroom at Vanderbilt. This university, along with other Southern schools such as UVA, is immensely proud of its Honor Code, which has always dictated the way in which its students behave. This Code grants students specific privileges in return for their honourable behaviour in examinations, paper guidelines and general living. Much quoted are the words of Madison Sarratt, one time dean of the university, 'Today I am going to give you two examinations, one in trigonometry and one in honesty. I hope you will pass them both, but if you must fail one, let it be trigonometry.' Regardless of whether students take these words as free licence to fail the dreaded maths class, every Vanderbilt student is proud of the trust that exists between the student body and the faculty.

It is the quality of this relationship between teacher and pupil that will determine how much you benefit from Vanderbilt's strong academic standing. While the reputation of this smaller and less prosperous university often suffers in comparison with the academic excellence boasted of by some of its East and West Coast contemporaries, it is actually more than capable of holding its own. The small class sizes (with a student–faculty ratio of 9:1) and the insularity of the campus offer students a real opportunity to form a relationship with their professors. While many of the faculty are genuinely interested in their pupils, the calibre of the lecturers covers a fairly wide range and students are advised to do their research before embarking on a particular course. Vandy has long been recognized as one of the top research universities in the Southern States and it has its fair share of academic superstars who know how to inspire their classes. However it is largely up to the student to seek them out. Students who accomplish this can be assured they are getting an education that will rival any of the more prestigious schools. Those who fail to do so may well find themselves frustrated.

Vanderbilt offers the standard liberal arts education to its students, requiring them to take a variety of core classes to broaden the base of their knowledge before they choose a specific area for concentration. These core areas include the humanities, sciences and mathematics and are covered by good introductory courses. The merits of Vanderbilt's academics have been shown by the increasing selectivity of its admissions process over recent years. As a result of this competition, would-be students need to think long and hard about their applications. The SAT I is required but unusually SAT IIs are not mandatory (although advised). This means that much rides on the personal statements and teacher recommendations that you provide. Early (binding) Decision is one option for those who have set their hearts on a place and there are a number of merit-based scholarships open to international students that are well worth enquiring about.

Williams

Williamstown, MA
www.williams.edu
2,000 undergraduates, 57 graduates

How many students does it take to change a light bulb at Williams? The whole student body – when you're snowed in, there's nothing else to do.

Williams is one of the few American colleges that draws only two reactions from its students – either they love it or they hate it. Fortunately, for the success of this small and thriving East Coast school, the majority of its undergraduates fall into the former category. But prospective students should be aware from the start that this is not a place for everyone. Situated in 450 acres in a tiny (as in one street) town in rural Massachusetts, Williams is an isolated college with superior academics and a small student body famed for having the nicest people around. Great for those who love skiing and sport, it could turn into a nightmare for anyone with a craving for crowds and the city lifestyle.

Since its foundation in 1793 (with the interesting objective of civilizing the local farm boys), Williams has prided itself on its unique liberal arts education. In some ways this school is more Ivy than the Ivies – in fact one of its most honoured traditions is that every graduating student plants some ivy! This is a fairly small college with only 2,000 Ephs (as they like to be known) at any one time and hugely strong faculty-student bonds. Excellent professors are constantly on hand and interested in what you have to say. Of course, when you are stuck in three foot of snow and you're fed up with all your roommates, tea with your professor seems like a great option and these bonds are one of the most exciting parts of the Williams' experience.

Williams operates on a term schedule that incorporates two long semesters and one month-long January semester where students can experiment by taking subjects pass/fail. The liberal arts core requirements consist of mandatory classes in the social sciences and natural sciences as well as the humanities. There is a certain expectation that Williams' students will want to pursue a broad education and the motivation of the preppy student body ensures that people make the most of their opportunities. Most of the undergrads are heading for careers in finance or grad school, where they have a hugely high success rate and their early ambitions stand them in good stead. This is shown by the fact that Williams is one of the colleges with proportionately the highest number of entries in the American *Who's Who*.

If you are not so turned on by the notion of money, consultancy or further years of education, you should also be aware that Williams offers some of the best art and music programmes in the country. It has long been noted for the mafia-like hold its alumni have over the art world, where they dominate as art critics, curators and historians. The fantastic museums and excellent art history teaching at Williams all contribute to the success of these graduates. Similarly, the proximity of the highly rated music school, Tanglewood, offers the concert pianists of the future a great place to study while getting their undergraduate degree.

All this success is not to say that Ephs do not know how to have fun. Although fraternities were banned in the 1960s and the 'going out' options are extremely limited, Williams has a reputation for being a beer-swilling party school. Known for the administration's willingness to turn a blind(ish) eye to alcohol consumption, on-campus parties tend to be frequent and well-attended. And for those who want to escape the drinking culture, the plethora of groups on campus (whenever people get bored, they are said to start another one) ensures that there is normally something else going on. The school's sporting prowess, which, despite its size is quite remarkable, also provides a chance for constant celebrations and the annual games against arch-rival Amherst turn out the entire student body.

In fact, it has been said that Williams is a school that attracts a certain type of preppy, wealthy, normally white and usually smart jock. Certainly this is a campus where you can expect to see a fair number of Brooks Brothers shirts and Abercrombie and Fitch sweaters. But diversity is creeping ever upwards and while jocks still take pride of place, the predominantly white factor is becoming ever less noticeable. Foreign students will also find they are welcomed with open arms – Williams is one of the few places that provides needs-blind financial aid to international as well as US citizens and is thus a great option for those worried about paying their tuition. 7% of the student body is international and Williams actively encourages its students to study abroad – ensuring the cosmopolitan perspective on campus is broader than just you! Many Brits might feel tempted to take advantage of the year abroad in Oxford programme, which truly offers you the best of both educational worlds.

Williams is one of those places it is important to check out in advance. While reports of it are almost always favourable, everyone admits it would not suit every individual. The campus and its architecture are undoubtedly beautiful and the students are reported to be the nicest people imaginable (and an incredibly bonded community), but the isolation and the limited socializing are a turn-off for many. Williams is 2+ hrs from Boston and 3 hrs from New York, and on long winter days, it can feel like it.

For those who love it, however, there can be no better college experience. The long-standing affection of Williams' graduates is aptly demonstrated by the fact that its alumni society is the oldest in America. Families continue to come here generation after generation (adding to its not undeserved WASP reputation). And Williams remains popular across the States – admitting only around 21% of all applicants. If you decide to become one of these, you need to make sure you get hold of the common application (the only one now used by Williams' admissions) and take the SAT I and three SAT IIs. And remember to talk to people and if possible visit, before you sign on that dotted line.

Famous Grads
James Garfield – President of the USA
Stephen Sondheim – composer
Dominick Dunne – gossip queen of *Vanity Fair*

Yale

New Haven, Connecticut
www.yale.edu
5,200 undergraduates, 2,300 graduates

How many students does it take to change a light bulb at Yale?
None – New Haven looks better in the dark.

Jewel. Muckheap. Two of the words that spring to mind when trying
to describe Yale and its local town, New Haven. Yet while the reasons
why one of the prettiest college campuses in the US ended up at the
centre of one of its ugliest industrial cities remain enigmatic, the
secret of the college's success are clear. This self-proclaimed
Oxbridge equivalent offers both American and international wun-
derkind a great academic experience, a social life that far surpasses
average Ivy Leagues and a name that is respected throughout the
world. And, something which even Harvard students agree on, it has
one of the coolest mascots around: the British bulldog!

The Campus

While the school itself started in 1701, it was not until 1718 that
Elihu Yale decided to follow in the footsteps of good old John
Harvard and build a monument to his own ego. A couple of book
donations later and the deal was struck. Enter the dreaming spires
of New England, brick buildings, grassy quads, an immense library
(for those original books) and a smattering of Gothic architecture.
Yale, the third oldest college in the nation, helped to set the well-
loved pattern for many other East Coast campuses. Its grounds are
both attractive and easy to navigate.

Yale follows in the footsteps of the Oxbridge tradition – random-
ly assigning each one of its students to one of the twelve residential

colleges. Each college has its own unique character and individual traditions are upheld with pride. Although most Yalies come to regard their college as the centre of their social activity, freshman year helps to establish connections across the community. While freshmen are aware of their house affiliation from the start, most initially live in the Old Campus. This location offers the best possible entrance to idyllic campus life – a collection of Gothic buildings situated around a quad designed for sunbathing or snowballing, depending on the season.

If Yale campus is the star, then New Haven is the foil by which it shines. Although intrepid and proud Yalies still swear that their surrounding metropolis is an interesting and safe place to explore, it offers few of the charms of Boston or Providence. Fortunately, for those students who crave the big city lights, New York is only an hour and a bit away by train – an easy weekend destination. And during the week? The immediate environs of the Yale campus are stocked with enough coffee shops, bars and restaurants to satisfy all but the most demanding student.

The Yalie

Both Yale and its longstanding rival, Harvard, have always considered themselves the intellectual homes of the New England elite. Since what Americans consider as the year dot, and we Brits consider as the eighteenth century, these colleges have been taking the brightest and the best (as well as the dimmest but most well-connected) of America's privileged families and putting them through their academic paces. Although much-needed egalitarianism has recently broadened the college intake, there are still many legacies pacing the campus. In your first few days at Yale, you may feel that every button-down shirted individual hails from Andover, Exeter, Groton or St Paul's – the American answer to Eton and Harrow.

Do not despair. Although you may still end up with a roommate whose name reads like the Mayflower passenger list (Lowell Eliot Winthrop Adams XII, for example), Yale, along with the other elite institutions, has been forced to curtail its blue blood intake in favour of brain cell count. The result? An extremely diverse group of students get to reap the profits provided by generations of wealthy elite. Yale today has a student class that is 30% minorities,

9% international and 54% public (for which read state) school educated. While the legacies continue – think the Bush dynasty – the
student body provides every possible cultural, ethnic and religious
outlet, and does so with a minimum of discrimination.

Yalies often boast about the friendliness of their school. And it
seems to be true. Despite the high pressure of academics and the
distinct social groups, most students pride themselves on their sense
of community. In part this may be attributed to the strong residential college programme – even in freshman year, students live within college groups. Yet, even discounting the bonds of accommodation, Yale students are a tolerant, cheerful and outgoing bunch.
There is a popular myth at Harvard that this sense of community
stems from the chip that all Yalies have on their shoulder – resulting
from their constant relegation to second best (in areas stemming
from the football field to such coveted academic prizes as the
Rhodes scholarship). Jealousy? Truth? Authorial objectivity prevents
comment, but you have been warned!

The Harvard–Yale rivalry is at its fiercest during the annual football game (held at Yale every other year). Despite the Bulldog's
recent losing streak (and the inconvenient situation of their football
stadium), sport is taken very seriously at Yale and there are over thir-
ty-five varsity teams. In fact, Yale is known for the support it gives to
extra-curricular activities. Yalies tend to be both energetic and ambitious. Whether writing for the oldest college daily, the *Yale Daily
News,* or pioneering the most obscure club around (the Ayn Rand
society, anyone?), many students devote infinitely more time to their
clubs, groups and associations than to class. After all who could turn
down the chance of joining an a cappella group known as the
Whiffenpoofs?

Some Yale students complain their schedules are simply too hectic and they have little time to simply enjoy being students. However,
most soon learn how to draw a happy medium between socializing,
academics and extra-curriculars. Once you have established your
personal pace, Yale provides an ideal environment for fulfilling your
dreams. The large endowment of the university means there is
always cash available to fund student projects and the faculty is generally interested in student well-being. Despite the prestige of the
school and the pressure of their academic lives, Yale kids tend to be

well-adjusted and happy individuals who benefit from the strong community that surrounds them.

Hitting the Books

Hooray for interested professors! The Yale community ethos extends to faculty as well as students. Yale recruits the brightest and the best in both departments and ensures they benefit from each other. The student–faculty ratio at Yale is under 7:1, and professors make a real effort to get to know their students. This is made much easier by the fact that Yale makes a concerted effort to keep its class sizes small – most of them under twenty students. This creates an experience more similar to the British tutorial experience and allows for some rewarding academic relationships. As at all American schools, classroom discussion is considered to be of the utmost importance and contributes significantly to one's grade. If you are the type of student who likes to sit quietly in the back of the room and snooze, then this may not be the environment for you.

Yale consists of the undergraduate college, a grad school and ten professional schools. When all of this academic energy is combined with a 10.7 billion dollar endowment, some pretty spectacular resources emerge. The libraries dominate the campus, both architecturally and otherwise. Yale possesses over 10.9 million bound books – a far cry from the handful initially donated by Elihu and others. Students may moan about the academic pressure, but at least it is done in the most comfortable surroundings with up-to-the-minute technology and the best professors that money (and the chance of tenure) can buy.

Yalies are spoilt for choice in their course selection, with over 2,000 options available. They also benefit from the infamous shopping period — a span of two weeks at the beginning of each semester where they can test as many classes as they like. The bane of every professor's existence, this trial period helps the students to weed out the most boring speaker and hardest reading load on campus. Harvard and Yale both share this custom along with the concept of reading week – a period before exams at the end of each semester which is allocated purely for revision purposes. This should not be underrated as a chance to catch up on that backlog of reading and to relax a little before the stress of finals.

The idea of a liberal arts education continues to form the core of Yale's attitude towards academics. The idea is that the student will teach him or herself how to learn and in so doing will form a foundation of knowledge that will prove valuable, whatever the unexpected turns of life. As such there is none of the specialization of English universities. While students have a major (the most popular are History, Economics and Political Science), they are also able to double major and are required to take courses in other areas.

These distributional requirements are similar to those at other schools. A language is considered necessary (French GCSE, anyone?) as well as selections from the humanities, social sciences and maths and science. Your major has a number of requirements as well. Yale students alternatively praise and bemoan the fact that Yale insists on thirty-six credits, rather than the customary thirty-two, for graduation. While it allows more flexibility, it also adds to the work load. Like all elite students, Yalies are not silent about these additional academic demands and competitions about who has the most work are commonplace. Yet this is after all the essence of the liberal arts education and, if you are making the trek to America, it is well worth pursuing.

Nor do you have to make the complicated decisions about which course to take on your own. All students are given freshman year advisers as well as later advisers who supervise their major. Both these and the faculty members themselves are always willing to give advice. While graduate students supervise many discussion classes, the faculty is very much present and encourages student communication.

Social Life
Yale, unlike other Ivy League schools, has woken up to the fact that 'all work and no play' makes for some very dull and unhappy students. Partly due to its strong sense of community and partly to the numerous local bars, restaurants and coffee houses, Yale students tend to enjoy a strong and diverse social life. While there is not the strong fraternity drinking culture that dominates many American schools, Yale students do not sit alone with their maths textbooks on a Saturday night. New Haven, despite its dubious qualities, offers the best pizza in New England (some say the world) at Sally's and Pepés

and a host of other cuisines to suit every taste. And after dinner, students have a variety of places to go on to – most notoriously the extremely-relaxed-on-IDs Toad's Place.

There are some clubs at Yale that are not accessible to all members of the campus. The secret societies, while not an integral part of everyone's Yale experience, are a fun aspect of its history. Dotted around the campus are huge, prison-like buildings with no discernable entrance. These are the secret societies – the most infamous of which is the Skull and Bones (the model for the 2000 film *The Skulls*). Although these societies are, by default, secret, it is generally known that men such as George W. Bush and John Kerry paced these halls in their senior years. Some of these societies are accessible to both men and women and their membership numbers are kept deliberately small. Initiation rites are also mysterious, candidates are 'tapped' at the end of their junior year and after that, who knows? While not for everyone, the presidential connection could be useful!

Outside Those Ivory Walls

For generations, Harvard students have returned from the annual football game, heaved huge sighs of relief and said, 'Thank goodness we don't live in New Haven'. Yalies, meanwhile, have fought to defend their local city, swearing that they wouldn't choose to live anywhere else. Both sides have some validity. New Haven, an industrial city with a high crime rate and acres of low-income, ghetto-like housing that circle the pleasant campus is not the most pleasant of New England destinations. Yet, largely helped by Yale, it has experienced something of a renaissance in recent years, its crime rate is falling and its prosperity growing.

While the boundaries between the immediate environs of the Yale campus and greater New Haven remain pretty much insurmountable, there has been an easing of campus–town relationships. Yale remains a very safe campus. Students have no shortage of places to shop, hang out and get caffeine fixes. And for the more serious, there are also a number of well-respected museums – note for Brits – the Yale Center for British Art is well worth an exploration. If you need even more cosmopolitan pursuits, New Haven is well-connected to New York and Boston by both train and bus.

If you are an active person, New Haven also offers great opportunities for hiking. Sleeping Giant State Park is close by and provides a nice escape from the confines of campus. The proximity of Yale to the Long Island Sound also means the water is near – something that provides both invigorating (read chilling) winter breezes and summer visits to the beach for those with cars. With all this on offer, the less salubrious parts of New Haven don't seem that bad.

Getting In

Yale and Harvard. Oxford and Cambridge. When names as renowned as these are thrown around you can be sure that the admissions process will not be a walk in the park. Yale is one of the most popular universities in America today and draws a huge number of applications. The administration states that it accepts almost 1,300 students out of 13,000 applicants, choosing those whom it believes will bring the most to the much-prized Yale community and make the most of its resources. The good news for Brits is that there has been a substantial attempt to internationalize the campus. The bad news is, it's still a very difficult process.

Yale does not try to hide the fact that it regards academics to be of primary importance. If your grades are poor, it is unlikely you will make the cut. Most SAT I results are in the low 700s and the incoming class is made up of students who have all been at the top of their high schools. Aside from the SAT I, the standard three SAT IIs are required. English students are at a big advantage here, however. Yale now also accepts completed A level results as a substitute for the SAT IIs (one A-Level for each test). This is extremely good news for those students who cannot find any SAT IIs that suit their sixth-form subject choices. However, you need to bear in mind that the results have to be completed before application, something which, unless you are taking a gap year, will probably not have happened. Academics aside, the Yale application form also requires two essays – your chance to show the admissions committee what you are made of.

Yale also recommends alumni interviews – available in London and other locations around the United Kingdom. While these are not essential, they come highly recommended. They allow the university to take a look at you (thus increasing your chances, unless you really irritate the interviewer) and, more importantly, they allow you to take a look at the university. This is the time to ask questions, probe the corners of Yale you might not know so well, and generally find out what you might be about to commit four years of your life to.

GOOD NEWS! Yale offers full financial aid on a needs-blind basis to international as well as American students. With the rises in English tuition fees and the crippling debt of UK student loans, the US plan, with the benefit of these extremely generous financial aid programmes, can actually make university in America a cheaper prospect. Definitely something to investigate.

Finally, Yale does offer an Early Action programme which enables students to express their preference for Yale above other schools. While the Early Action programme still allows Regular Decision application to other universities, you are no longer able to apply early to anywhere other than Yale. So you need to be fairly set on the idea, and fairly organized, to follow this route.

Famous Grads

George Bush (1 and 2) – could recent grad Barbara Bush be next in line?

Cole Porter — delicious and de-lovely

Eli Whitney – if you don't know who this is now, you will in four years' time

On Your Way – Almost!

So you have decided to give the US a go? Read on for some advice on how to jump the next set of hurdles!

How to Deal with Long-Distance Family

Sending your child off to university is a big deal for any parent. As soon as the 'Thank God I have the house/car/fridge to myself' mentality has worn off, the 'Why is my little darling so far away?' line of thought steps in. If the little darling in question has decided that the best place to fly the parental nest to is America, then all the normal fears, worries, and paranoia are multiplied by a factor of ten. Even if the mother or father in question is in fact American or has experienced the college system first hand, the thought of the Atlantic dividing them from emergency laundry help can cause a fair amount of hysteria. The trick for the child is in learning how to handle this as it arises.

Probably the first rule of thumb for allaying the anxious parent's fears is to invest in a good phonecard or international dialling deal and make sure you remember to call home on a semi-regular basis. Also rest assured that American universities are much better than their English equivalents at managing parents. From the flow of information that will start to stream in before freshman year, to organized weekends specifically designed to allow the parents to actually see what their precious child is getting up to, the college administration really tries to make families feel involved. In so doing, they take much of the pressure off the child.

You should also remember that LA is about the same distance from the East Coast as London is from New York and that many of your American classmates will endure similar homesickness and anxious parents. In fact, when yours are driving you round the bend, you will normally find the same is true for those of your friends whose parents live just down the road. In many ways having family members a good 3,000 miles away is good for all concerned (take note of the following points and use them to allay maternal fears). Family relationships are often improved by distance and your parents and siblings will love the fact they now have a built-in American shopper to find them Levi jeans and Reese's peanut butter cups. You, meanwhile, will find the odd visitor from home is exceedingly welcome. After all, who else can you prevail upon to smuggle in such banned delicacies as Marmite and Cadburys? Furthermore as an 'American orphan' you have the chance to impose yourself on your roommates, families allowing you both to capitalize on pity for your abandoned status and to explore whole new aspects of the States.

One of the things most parents worry about when their child flies across the pond is their social life. Will all their friends be American? Will they lose touch with their English peers and prefer to spend their holidays in far-flung corners of the States? In fact, for most English students, the opposite will prove true. American students love to travel and little ol' Europe is number one on their list of destinations. Brits studying in the States are more likely to find themselves operating as a backpacking hostel during the holidays, than sitting at home alone. Americans love England and you will never have any shortage of visitors.

Nor, in spite of your family's anxiety should you have any problems in maintaining your English friendship groups. Your school contemporaries may well drift apart as they go to different universities and form new English friendship groups, but you should (with minimal effort) be able to become the link between them all. The fact that you will not be making hundreds of new friends in England means you are forced to make that little bit more of an effort with the old ones and normally it pays off. Now that phone calls and plane tickets are so cheap, it is easy to stay in contact with all your loved ones, regardless of which side of the Atlantic you happen to be on. And with a little bit of luck, you should be able to emerge from your undergraduate years with solid friendship groups (who have even, shock horror, grown to like each other) on both sides of the pond.

For the Parents

It's also time to give your parents something to think about. Show them this.

Your main role as a parent is to be supportive – and support will be needed in bucketloads. Getting to university in the US is a drawn-out process with a raft of requirements – and all the while your child is bogged down in the middle of a battlefield of A levels. To venture to another country for university is brave and nerve-wracking for everyone involved, so share the excitement of one of the most significant experiences your child will have - and keep the application show on the road.

There are over 4,000 universities and colleges in the US, so tracking down the institution best suited to your child can be daunting. You can begin whittling down the selection process by asking your child the following questions:

1 What types of activity would you like to see on a campus?
2 What do you want to achieve by studying in the US?
3 Would you be happier in an urban, suburban or rural environment?
4 Would you prefer a small college, with only a few hundred students, or a large university with thousands of students?
5 Which climate is more appealing to you outside the UK?

Last, and most important:
6 Ask yourself what kind of budget you have for your child studying in the US.

The Fulbright recommends you take three sheets of paper and head them First Choice, Second Choice and Safety. Safety institutions are those to which your child feels sure of entry because their achievements exceed the admission requirements. These lists will help you to identify what is within your child's reach. Try to be as encouraging as possible about every institution your child zeros in on. Identify the differences between institutions and pin down what makes them interesting. Then match them to the criteria you have generated above.

Application to a US university is technical and time-consuming. Study this book carefully – you will probably see ramifications of the various requirements which your child will not.

To set out these requirements briefly:

Admission to US universities is based on academic merit and standardized tests. Personal recommendations and extra-curricular activities also count. The application process takes a long time. If your child wants to begin studying in September 2007, it's vital to get the ball rolling in early 2006.

The first step is to contact the universities which your child is actively considering. The application form usually consists of a questionnaire about academic and cultural background. It is important to answer all questions honestly and accurately. Your child will also need an official copy of their academic record (or 'transcript') – not something most UK schools are used to providing, so give them plenty of time and information. Letters of recommendation – references, but not as we know them – will be needed, too, written by a teacher or employer who knows the applicant's character and work. Check with the institutions to which your child is applying and see if recommendations should be sent separately. Make sure the person writing them understands what is needed (see page 219).

Money Matters

The key to financial planning is to start early so you and your child can keep on top of the many challenges. You must be fully aware of the financial commitment involved in studying abroad. Most US students have low-interest government loans. As a UK resident you are only able to apply for a US loan if you have an American co-signer. Encourage your child to believe that funding an education abroad is attainable. It's a long and winding road, and parents are definitely needed on the journey.

The non-refundable application fee for each university ranges from $20 to $150 and covers only the processing cost. Some universities require applicants to cover international mailing costs, and/or charge for prospectuses. A visa will be granted only if a student can prove they have sufficient funds to cover all costs for the first year. It is difficult to generalize the basic cost of an academic year because institutions set their own tuition fees and the cost of living varies greatly according to location. Tuition runs anywhere from $4,000 to $50,000 per academic year (nine months). Students must buy their books, adding as much as $1,000 a year to the cost. Living expenses are highest in big cities, ranging from $5,000 to $16,000 a year. You will also need to factor in air travel to and from the US along with health insurance and personal spending money.

The best source of funding for your child's US education is the institution itself. Many of them allocate funds for international students, mostly based on academic merit, though some colleges offer funding based on need. Usually, more funding is available from private rather than state institutions; however, full scholarships are rare. It requires a huge amount of time to research and apply for scholarships. Funding from independent bodies is less common, but it is available. Some universities give athletic or performing arts scholarships. It is extremely important if your child wants to apply for a scholarship to be certain the scholarship is available to international students.

A student visa allows on-campus work for up to twenty hours per week to help cover living expenses and to earn pocket money. But note, none of this income can count towards a visa application. Help your child research and draw up a budget. Is it affordable? How does it compare with the costs of university in the UK? Is the difference in quality really worth it?

Health and Safety

One common concern for a parent thinking of sending their child overseas is safety. Rest assured, American colleges (ever wary of lawsuits) take very good care of their students. Most campuses have security staff or police who patrol day and night. Many have an escort service to pick students up and drive or walk them to any destination on or around campus. These services are usually free and operate until late. Most institutions have emergency call boxes located around campus which directly access police emergency lines. Find out what security services are available and make sure your child will be able to call an escort when needed, or walk with a friend.

In case of an emergency it is extremely important your child has not left home without as many means of contact as possible. Email addresses, mailing addresses, phone numbers of family members and fax numbers are just some of the suggested safety contacts. It will be up to you to talk to your child about what means of communication to use and in what order. Most universities have a parent support network with a designated person to help deal with international students and parents. Before your child makes a definite decision on a university, check the services each institution's International Student Office (ISO) provides.

Insurance

International students need to check with the campus health centre to see if their insurance policy will be affordable and suitable. Services vary depending on the size and location of the institution. Some campus health centres offer emergency care, others don't. Contact your centre direct, or the International Student Office, to find out more. Some institutions require international students to take out their own health cover.

Carefully look at the range of insurance plans available from both the UK and the US to establish which offer the best value for money and the most comprehensive coverage. A perfect health insurance policy covering 100% of the costs for 100% of the time may be too expensive. One which covers the majority of costs may, of course, leave you picking up the tab for the shortfall.

There are significant differences between US and UK healthcare policies. You must weigh up the advantages and disadvantages, and plump for the one tha's best for you. Principal differences are cost, preventive healthcare, pre-existing conditions and liability insurance. Some student cards offer limited insurance cover. For example, the International Student Identity Card (ISIC) is a globally recognized identification card which carries some insurance benefits.

Communication

Communicating with your child throughout the application process in the UK is crucial. Make time to talk regularly about how it's going.

It is a good idea to contact other students who have studied abroad and discuss the realities of living there, including funding, academic life and cultural lifestyle. These people are an incredibly valuable source of information and contacts can be found through the Internet or the International Student Office of the institution your child will be attending. The ISO also provides other services for your child once they are in the US, usually including culture shock therapists and counsellors.

What Do I Do and When?

Follow this timeline and you cannot go wrong. (And bear in mind this is for the super-organized. These things can be done in much less time if you are of the more chaotic variety!)

American university years begin, like ours, in September. Start the process at least *eighteen* months before you expect to enrol. So:

January–June Get the preliminaries out of the way. Why do you want to study in the US? Which is the right university for you? Take your time – applying to a US uni is challenge enough without applying to the wrong one. Will you need financial aid? What are the application/financial aid deadlines for your chosen universities? SATs have to be taken in advance. Make sure you register for them in time. Talk to your school/college – many of them will have experience of leaping the hurdles you face.

August Write to universities for application and financial aid forms/catalogues. Obtain test registration forms to sit the SAT

(Reasoning Test) and if necessary SAT Subject Tests.

September–December Ask your school for an 'official transcript'. Ask your teachers for letters of recommendation. Submit applications for admission and financial aid. Check that transcripts and references have arrived. Sit the necessary admissions tests.

January–April There will be various application deadlines which you must meet.

April–June Letters of acceptance or rejection will arrive. Pinpoint which university to attend, notify them of your decision, complete and return any forms they require. Send letters of regret to those universities you reject. Organize finances (arrange to transfer funds to a US bank; make sure you have funds for travel and expenses on arrival). Finalize arrangements for housing and medical insurance with your university.

July Apply to the American Embassy for a visa as soon as you get the I20 form from your chosen university (see Visa section below). Make travel arrangements. Contact the International Student Office at your university with details of your arrival plans.

August–September Start packing! And enjoy yourself.

Confused by the jargon? Daunted by having to do all this yourself rather than letting your school gently guide you through UCAS? Read on – all will be explained.

The Application Procedure
Basic requirements

The least you need to apply to a US university is five GCSEs, or Scottish Standard Grades, at C or above in core subject areas, including English and maths – a hurdle you will leap lightly over. This is not to say that at the age of sixteen, laurelled with five Cs, you will be welcomed with open arms by Harvard. All universities normally want a student to be eighteen and above, unless there are very unusual circumstances, and most universities will want to see post-sixteen attainment too: generally two to three A levels or equivalent (International Baccalaureate (IB), Scottish Highers, BTEC, GNVQs, AVCEs). All of these will be considered, but it is important to check with individual universities to see what their minimum standards for admission are. IB in particular is well understood. In rare cases you may need to pay to have your qualifications evaluated – see the Reference Section for companies that will do this.

Most students will be applying at the beginning of the second year of sixth form for a place the following Autumn term. Because of this, universities will scrutinize GCSE and AS/Highers results together with predicted A2/IB/Highers marks. However, unlike British universities, acceptance will not be dependent on your A2, etc. results. Don't think this enables you to do nothing for your final year. You also have to face the challenge of the American Scholastic Aptitude Tests (more simply known as the SAT) or its cousin the ACT.

Dealing with the SAT

Most universities will require you to take an admissions test. The most popular exam is the SAT Reasoning Test. This was once known as the SAT I but is now commonly referred to as the SAT. More competitive universities may also want you to take SAT Subject Tests (known as SAT IIs until 2004). Many universities also accept the ACT (A.C.T.) in place of the SAT.

Don't worry too much. You are an international student and, despite the official line, colleges will not expect you to do as well in these exams as Americans. Any American with the hope of applying for a prestigious college has been in SAT training for years, coached through courses, put through numerous practices and schooled to within an inch of their lives. British and other international students frequently walk in on the day of the exam and take it cold.

Universities understand our academic background does not, for the most part, incorporate standardized testing. Providing GCSE, AS level and A level predictions are of a sufficiently high standard, slightly lower grades on these American exams are, if not discounted, partially excused.

The average British student writes their way through school-essays for GCSE, more essays for AS levels, yet more essays for A levels.

Meanwhile the average American student completes high school in a blaze of ticked boxes and filled bubbles – the standardized testing process of SATs. The tendency among many Brits is to dismiss such multiple choice testing as ridiculous. Yet for the indefinite future every international student with aspirations to American colleges has no option but to submit to these exams, regardless of their academic background.

The format of SATs may be more straightforward than their English equivalent but this does not mean you can treat them disdainfully. Competition for the prestigious American universities to which most British students aspire is fierce, and SATs are a significant hurdle that all must leap. You will need scores of over 600 for your application even to be considered at the top institutions.

The cold hard facts

Plan ahead! You need to register for your SATs about two months in advance of the exam date. The easiest way to do this is online at *www.collegeboard.com* (*www.actstudent.org* for the ACT). The process is lengthy but simple and reserves you a seat and paper for a specific date. There is a charge for taking these exams – around $50 for the SAT itself (the Reasoning Test) and $16 (plus registration) for each SAT Subject Test. This can be paid online when registering.

SATs are offered half a dozen times a year at a surprisingly large number of places around the UK so it is pretty easy to find a nearish test centre. All sites are listed on *www.collegeboard.com* – a website that together with *www.princetonreview.com* may well become your SAT bible.

Unless you are aiming for a nervous breakdown, don't take all these exams at once. The SAT Reasoning Test (or the ACT if this is your preferred exam) is the most challenging for many Brits and is best dealt with first. You can start taking it the year after your GCSEs. The more specialized Subject Tests are straightforward compared with their A level equivalents and involve less preparation. You can fit them in at a slightly later date.

You can take SATs and ACTs repeatedly with very little bother – a situation many A level students long for. However the universities will be notified of all the SAT/ACT grades you have ever achieved, not just the sparkling 1600 you obtained in your latest attempt, so it will look distinctly strange if your early scores fall out of the range your university would hope to see. It is much better to invest time in practising beforehand – there are lots of test preparation materials as well as tutors available. (See the Reference Section at the back of the book, and our recommendations on practice materials on page 212.) Common sense should tell you when to quit. Most Brits find that one attempt is in fact enough to secure a satisfactory grade.

When you register for the exam you have the option of sending your scores directly to colleges of your choice. If you don't know where you wish to apply, just leave this blank. When you make up your mind later, it is easy to contact the scoreboard and send the official copy of the results to the colleges you are looking at. But if you do have your heart set on a particular college from the word go, sending the scores directly will save you time and trouble at a later date.

The format of the SAT

The SAT (Reasoning Test) focuses on writing, critical reading and mathematics. The total testing time is 3 hours and 45 minutes.

The writing section measures your ability to develop and support an argument on a topic as well as your ability to recognize errors and make improvements to given pieces of writing (multiple choice). The total testing time is 60 minutes: 25 for the essay and 35 for the multiple choice section. The score range for the writing section is 200 to 800.

The critical reading section measures your ability to identify genre, relationships between parts of a text, cause and effect, rhetorical devices and comparative arguments. The passages are chosen from a variety of academic areas. There are three multiple-choice sections (two 25-minute sections and one 20-minute section). The score range for the critical reading section is 200 to 800.

The mathematics sections incorporate algebra and functions, geometry, statistics, probability and data analysis. There are three multiple-choice sections (two 25-minute sections and one 20-minute section). The score range for the mathematics section is 200 to 800.

Beyond getting some practice at the unusual format (see below) you will need to feel confident of your grasp of English (particularly the niceties of grammar!). Your maths will also have to be up to a good AS level standard. If you dropped it with relief after GCSEs it may be wise to ask for specific tuition from your school – or find a private tutor.

SAT Subject Tests

You cannot take the SAT (Reasoning Test) and SAT Subject Tests on the same day. Subject Tests cover a wide range of subjects and are more akin to A levels – while still, amazingly, being almost entirely multiple choice. They last an hour and you can take more than one at the same sitting. They are more clear-cut than their A level equivalents, much shorter, and involve less preparation for Brits who are used to concentrating on one subject at a time. If your university requires you to take the Subject Tests, check with them to see if there are required subjects you must sit or if you have free choice in what to take.

There are twenty Subject Tests including: Literature, US History,

World History, Math Level 1, Math Level 2, Biology E/M, Chemistry, Physics, French, French with Listening, German, German with Listening, Spanish, Modern Hebrew, Italian, Latin, Japanese with Listening, Korean with Listening and Chinese with Listening. Watch out. In some of these languages the standard will be set by the many US native speakers, and in others the curriculum may not be what you have covered in the UK – do your homework. The score range is 200 to 800.

ACT

The ACT is given five times a year at many locations throughout the UK. It is a multiple-choice exam which measures English, Mathematics, Reading and Sciences Reasoning. On each of the four tests you will receive a raw score. This raw score will be converted to a scaled score from 1 to 36, and your combined score will be the average of your four scaled scores.

SAT Reasoning Test or ACT?

With a very few exceptions, US universities accept both these tests and treat them the same. In their current formats, the ACT is broader than the SAT Reasoning Test, covering more ground to less depth, and will be more in tune with your own education. Many schools, though, have experience of getting pupils through SATs but not the ACT, and SAT is the more common test for international students to take. Any requirement to sit SAT Subject Tests will apply whichever of the SAT Reasoning Test or ACT you have taken.

Getting the results

The dreaded results are available by phone or on the web around three weeks after the exam. They are then sent on to colleges requested at the time of the test.

Fear not

There are many companies making a great deal of money out of coaching students through the SAT. And as the number of Brits interested in applying to US schools has risen, so have the resources available on this side of the pond. Even though the vast majority of British schools have no concept of what SATs actually are, there are now a variety of other options for those students who decide they need coaching. These range from hours of one-on-one tuition to huge coaching guides available on the high street (see Reference Section). Students can also sign up for courses with others preparing for the test (see Reference Section). In reality, although there are a few useful shortcut methods, you may find the best way of improving your scores is simply to practise multiple-choice tests in timed conditions. So buy a guide with a number of different sample tests and back-of-the-book answers, grab a stopwatch and get down to work. See our recommended list on p. 247.

Words to the wise

GET THESE EXAMS OUT OF THE WAY. There are two reasons for this. First, if you are a baffled Shakespeare buff who gladly burnt all your maths textbooks after the rigours of GCSE, the compulsory Math SAT Reasoning Test may inspire panic. Don't let it! Face this dreaded test – and the additional tutoring you may require – as soon as possible after the actual maths GCSE. In this way you can put your extensive knowledge of quadratic equations to good use before it flies forever. Just don't forget your calculator!

Second, even if your heart is set on the US, your A level exams are still going to be important to you later, and perhaps even more so to your parents. You do not want to be taking SATs at the same time as AS/A levels, vital coursework or mock examinations. As the exams are offered so regularly it is easy to schedule them for a relatively fallow period. And once you've done them, you'll have the reassuring knowledge that you at least have some solid exam results behind you as you head into the A levels!

Take a timed practice test in advance. Three hours of checking boxes is very different from three hours of essay writing. It may feel as if you have masses of time but it rushes past deceptively quickly. For the verbal section you need to complete around seventy-eight questions in 35 minutes; for maths about sixty in 75 minutes. This is a pretty fast rate of work and not one for which A level preparation will be of any help.

Once you've started your exam, you HAVE to keep going. Each question is only worth a small number of points, so there is no sense in spending hours on one problem only to run out of time on five you could have knocked off easily. Getting a question wrong costs you a quarter of a point. Getting one right earns you a full point. Leaving it blank does nothing to your score, so cutting your losses and ploughing on regardless is essential.

Each section of the test gets harder as you move through it. If you are faced with a question you think you cannot answer, try to eliminate the options that are definitely wrong. This will narrow your choice. Go with your instincts. If your instincts have chosen this precise moment to vanish, move on. Just make sure you leave the corresponding bubble blank.

When you're taking these multiple-choice tests, make sure you don't make the fatal mistake of accidentally skipping a question and carrying on regardless. Filling out seventy-five answers in the wrong bubble is ridiculously easy to do and will be catastrophic for your score. As you go, check your answers are in line with the questions.

The different methods, curricula and subject matter taught in US schools can make it difficult to pin down suitable SAT Subject Tests. For example, an A level Biology syllabus may have a very different focus from that of high school AP biology. History presents even more of a problem – the Tudors and the Stuarts have little place even in the World History exam. Your best bet is to go for the English literature exam (which some schools actually require). It is also useful to do a language exam (though the questions may be more grammatically based than we are used to). Many universities have a foreign language requirement and sometimes a high enough score on the Subject Tests will enable you to skip it. Taking French, Spanish, or even Latin can help you kill two birds with one stone.

People customarily arrive for their SATs with around twenty-five different pencils, rubbers, sharpeners, etc. Truckloads of stationery may be excessive but do make sure you have spares. And in case you're wondering what on earth a no. 2 pencil is — an HB will suffice.

Keep copies of your scores. Even though your university will have them somewhere on file, you may well need to produce them in the future in order to fulfil certain academic requirements. It saves a huge amount of hassle and expense if you have them handy. (The same holds true for A level certificates – all academic results can help you find ways around tricky courses you might otherwise be required to take at a later date.)

If English is not your native language, you may have to take the Test Of English As A Foreign Language (TOEFL). This is true even if you have spent years studying in the UK. It doesn't make sense, but sometimes they still make you do it. If you think you may need to take this exam, go to *www.toefl.org* for further information.

Applications

Once you have selected your universities, contact them directly to obtain an application form. Most of these forms are online and many will allow you to submit electronically (saving on that international postage!). Approximately 200 of them use 'The Common Application Form' (see *www.commonapp.org*), which is a great way to get around what is otherwise a huge amount of work. However, there may still be additional requirements from specific universities and, unlike UCAS, each university will require you to submit a separate application and fee.

Each application requires a personal statement. Unlike the UCAS form, where you do not discuss individual institutions, US universities will want to know why you want to attend their school in particular. Americans tend not to be reticent about their personal achievements, and you should not hold back out of any false or British modesty. Make sure your prospective university really knows about how wonderful you are, how much you want to attend their school and what a benefit you will be to their student body. Each personal statement will need to be targeted for a particular school – so be sure you put them in the right envelopes! Personal statements for US universities will typically be much longer than UCAS versions so you have a chance to put all your best qualities on display. Make sure other people read it through for typos, grammar and other suggestions before you send it in.

In addition to the application and standardized test results, many universities will require one or more essays. It is crucial you take your time over these essays as they are often the deciding factor in admission. Each university is trying to suss out if you will fit in, and if the hard data (test scores/grades) is not quite at the required standard, or if the competition is hot, your essays could sway the decision. These essays tend to be in response to a vaguely worded question about your values, your interests or your most significant experiences and while the whole thing may seem a bit pretentious, its value should NOT be underestimated. Make sure you write on things that are unique, interesting and informative about you. And pick something you're interested in – the essay will read much better if you have some conviction when you're writing it. Again, each college will be looking for candidates that suit them, so remember to target each essay individually.

There are many organizations such as EAS and Petersons that provide essay review services and, depending on your circumstances, these may be worth the cost. American publishers have also cottoned on to the anxious parent markets and books with titles like *100 Successful Harvard/Yale/Stanford College Essays* are available. The one we recommend is *Peterson's Best College Admission Essays* (see p. 247).

Recommendations

Each university will ask you for at least two recommendations. These should typically come from your head teacher, careers adviser, personal tutor or any teachers who know you well. Once again, they are very important and it is crucial you make sure your referee knows the drill. While some admissions officers appreciate British understatement, you are competing for a place against American students whose references will tend to be flagrantly positive, so it is wise to give the person you ask some guidance.

For Referees – What to include in your recommendations

Be assertively affirmative! US referees focus tightly on achievements and blur less desirable qualities. Make a list with your student of all the main reasons they wish to study in the US and draw upon it.

If necessary, explain discrepancies in grades, i.e. those due to ill health or personal problems. This will make the student's own explanation more credible.

Include all extra-curricular activities. Admissions officers badly want students who will contribute to campus life, not just excel in a main topic of study. Five As at AS Level are great but that position in the school orchestra could prove just as valuable.

Highlight the student's personality. Many applicants with less than perfect marks have been accepted by top-rated institutions because they will contribute to the diversity of the student body, be a team-player or an enthusiastic member of campus.

Try to offer a class ranking. Most US high schools assign their students to various percentiles based on academic ability. You can be inventive and selective: for example, a student in the top 40% of their year-group may be in the top 3% for their favourite subject. Consider using the ranking in the last GCSE year if students leaving have made the AS rankings a steeper slope to climb.

Don't hold back. US referees often use highly descriptive, dramatic language. Paint an honest portrait in full colour. In the US a reference is viewed as a marketing tool. You should try to do the same.

Examples of references

In order to demonstrate some of the (not so) subtle differences between references, Samantha Crowie of the Fulbright's US–UK Educational Advisory Service has created a student-written summary of their qualifications and activities, together with two supporting references, one UK-style, the other US-style. Each takes its national style to the extreme, but we hope they will show you the way to making your reference more US-friendly.

Joe Normal has GCSE results of A* in English Literature; A in English Language and History; B in Maths, Science, Art and IT; C in French and Music; D in D&T. At AS he has A in English Literature, B in History, C in Art and Biology. He is predicted A in English Literature, B in History, C in Art at A2.

Joe plays football for his school team. Last year he played in the city finals, where his team lost the championship. He plays the clarinet in the school wind band. His work group in GCSE Science won a regional award for their energy-efficient car design. Over the summer holidays he participated in a week-long art workshop organized by his school for local children. He recently completed his silver Duke of Edinburgh Award, hoping to take the Gold before leaving school. He won a Promising Young Writers Award for a short story written as part of his GCSE coursework.

The US universities he is applying to (majoring in English) are

Middlebury, Harvard, NYU, Mount Holyoake, College of William and Mary, and Northeastern.

Example of a UK-style reference

Joe Normal is a very likeable student with a solid future ahead of him. He interacts well with his classmates and seems to be quite popular among his peers.

Academically, he achieves decent marks and has good relationships with his teachers, although he could be more focused upon deadlines. He should have a great future in the study and application of English, which is by far his favourite subject, and the field in which he is most gifted.

Joe demonstrates a certain willingness to participate in school events such as music concerts, and recently supervised a group of six young children engaged in various art-based activities on one of our summer schemes. His work with the Duke of Edinburgh Awards scheme also proves his ability to overcome challenges.

I would have no reservations in recommending Joe for your institution, and am sure he will become a considerable academic asset.

Example of a US-style reference

It has been an absolute pleasure to work with Joe Normal, who ranks among the top 10% of students within his A level classes.

He is the best student in a competitive and enthusiastic English class, and has even won a publisher's Young Writers Award for one of the pieces he produced. His passion for the subject shines through, as does his commitment to learning in an academic setting.

Joe stands out as a popular team player, both in his school work and extra-curricular activities, taking his soccer team to the city championships, and winning a science award for a group project on environmental awareness. While working towards his Duke of Edinburgh Silver Award he endured a two-day mountaineering expedition, and returned with much praise for the challenge, and is anticipating another such trek for his soon-to-be-completed Gold Award.

He is keen to participate by playing his clarinet at regular wind band concerts, and has recently taken time out of his school holiday to volunteer with the art department, supervising workshops for local children.

Joe's teachers speak highly of him, and all predict he will be extremely successful in a US institution, where his academic talents can continue to flourish, and his love of adventure will be greatly rewarded. I do not hesitate to give my strongest recommendation that he join 'x' University and am certain you will be rewarded with an exemplary new student.

Transcripts

Your school will need to provide a transcript of your academic record from Year 10 to the present. This is not something that is customary in the UK and most schools will have to create this document from scratch. Make sure you explain the situation to your teachers in good time and show them the following explanation for the sake of clarification.

A US transcript typically consists of a list of grades that high school students have received in every class in which they have ever been enrolled. The following is based on suggestions from US university admissions officers and administrators. Use it as a guide only – read the application information or contact the admissions office for each individual university to learn about specific requirements.

A special note to teachers and careers advisers

US universities are less interested in students' final exam results than in the subjects they have taken over the last four years and how their performance has changed over time. A US transcript lists courses taken by semester with the grades for each course. (US schools divide the school year into two semesters, as opposed to the UK three-term system.) If possible, admissions officers appreciate a similar document from UK schools for the sake of comparison.

For many schools, this will be a tedious exercise involving trawling through dusty student records. Please do your very best – it makes a real difference to your student's chances, and US universities really do want a clear picture of how they have done in every term in every subject over the last four years.

If your school does not give grades on a term basis, any type of evaluatory mark is acceptable. Include a note explaining the grading system used. An example of this might be: 'Each mark reflects an individual instructor's assessment of the student's coursework, including homework, tests, class participation and final examinations. Each grade is on a scale of A to F, where A is excellent, C is satisfactory, and F is failing.'

After the internal marks, set out the examination results obtained over that period – and not just the main ones: CLAIT, RSA too. Then list the other, non-examined courses pursued: Enrichment, General Studies or whatever. Don't leave anything out.

These documents should be on an official school letterhead, with a school stamp of certification if possible.

A special note to applicants

If you have certified copies of your qualifications (GCSEs, etc.), enclose them with your application. If you do not, you need to obtain copies from each of the examining boards in plenty of time. Also bear in mind you should get a transcript from all secondary schools or sixth form colleges you have attended.

Interviews

Although interviews are rarely mandatory for admission into any American university, they are often recommended and are an excellent way of finding out about the place in which you are planning to spend the next four years. Interviews for international students can function in two ways. If you are embarking on the grand college trip (a whistle-stop tour around ten colleges in five days), it is advisable you try to meet with people in the admissions offices while you're on campus. They'll be impressed that you,re organized enough to make the effort and it is a good chance to get any questions about the place cleared up while you're still on site. If personal interviews aren't available you should still attend the tours and sessions for applicants. These people have got selling their institution down to a fine art and it would be a shame to miss out on the spiel.

The other and more common way of interviewing is via the alumni systems many colleges have set up. American universities believe that no one is more qualified to judge an applicant than one who has been there and survived. The majority of the top universities recommend these interviews and since their alums tend to be flung far and wide, there are normally many eager Americans in London just waiting to find the perfect Brit for their alma mater. Preparation for these interviews need not be extensive – although wearing the colour of your intended school is one possible starting point! In general, these alumni are as intent on selling their school as they are on screening you and this is the best time to ask all those questions the many guides on your bookshelves have left uncovered. In most cases these interviews have very little sway in the application process but are a great opportunity to form one more bond with the school and find out what you really want to know. Don't stress about them too much, just brush your hair, put on your best English manners and be prepared to talk about why you're interested in America and what you hope to get out of your university experience there.

And in case you're wondering, the university will make sure that its interviewers in England get in touch with you. So don't start pestering them, every adequate applicant will get an interview, but sometimes matching up assignments can take a while.

Financial Statement

Most universities will require you to complete a financial statement. Do this carefully as it will be used to determine your eligibility for financial assistance. Do not worry that it may affect the decision to accept you - it will not! At undergraduate level, the decision to offer a place is completely separate from an offer of financial aid. US universities, admission decisions are based on merit, not ability to pay.

Deadlines

Meet your deadlines! US universities will not accept late applications unless they have 'rolling admissions', meaning they accept students on a first-come, first-served basis. Most deadlines occur between January and February, although they can be as early as November and as late as March. You must send your university everything they ask for, all of it in perfect order (follow the instructions very carefully!) well before the deadline. The date posted counts for nothing: if you are close to a deadline send your application by an express service that will require a signature on delivery.

And the good news will generally arrive in April.

Early Decision/Early Action

Students who have planned well in advance and are keen to attend a particular university may wish to consider ŒEarly Decision/Early Action'.

Early Action is a non-binding plan that requires students to submit their applications in early autumn. Notification of acceptance is made by January, but students have until 1 May to accept or reject the offer. The advantage is you will know much earlier and can plan accordingly. The disadvantage is that candidates who apply this way tend to be much stronger and rejection is more likely than in the regular admission pool.

Early Decision is a binding plan following the same timescale as Early Action. By applying this way, you have made a commitment, should you be accepted, to attend the university. You can only choose one university to apply as an Early Decision candidate. Reneging on an offer of admission could mean that no other university will admit you, so make sure your heart is absolutely set on this college before you send off the forms.

To consider either of these plans, you will need to be clearly focused and will need to prepare well in advance.

Students with Additional Needs

America makes students with additional needs very welcome, and strong (rather stronger than in the UK) laws ensure they are not discriminated against. If you have any type of disability or Special Educational Needs, make sure you tell the university from the start and that they can accommodate you. While most US universities are very adept at catering for disabled students and can normally provide an array of services, there may be additional costs – contact the university's student services division for further information. As you will have to provide evidence of your disability, and the requirements differ from the UK, it is wise to start asking two years before you plan to enrol.

Practice Materials

It will be worth your while to buy your own personal copies of study guides for the exams you have chosen to take. You can then work through these in your own time at home. You will find a multitude of them listed on the websites in the Reference Section, or on *Amazon.com* (some even on *Amazon.co.uk*).

Our recommendations are:

For the SAT
College Board's *The Official SAT Study Guide*, £15
Peterson's *SAT Online Practice Tests*, £50

For the ACT
Peterson's *Master the ACT Assessment 2005*, with CD, £15
Peterson's *ACT Online Practice Tests*, £50

General
Peterson's *Best College Admission Essays*, £10
Things to Know Before You Go, from the US–UK Fulbright Commission, £5

Prices are indicative. You can buy these from a wide variety of sources, including the US–UK Fulbright Commission, but check out our website *www.uniintheusa.com* – we aim to be cheaper than anyone else (once you have factored in the postage from the US).

Money Matters 2
Athletic scholarships
Always wanted to be a jock? Here's how ...

Every American high school movie worth its salt is guaranteed to have at least one 'jock' in a starring role. These mini-gods of the athletic field are invariably blessed with the best-looking cheerleader as their girlfriend, the adulation of their peers, and perfect floppy hair. British athletes may have missed out on this high school experience, but American university offers them a second chance. Those of you with enough sporting talent may still have the opportunity to capture some of this limelight while also earning sizeable help with the application process and subsequent tuition fees.

American universities (even the smaller and more academic ones) consider sport to be one of the most important ingredients in their curriculum. While it is unlikely a Brit is going to land the quarterback position on the UMichigan American football team, there are many sporting areas in which we do excel (or at least rival Americans). Crew (rowing) teams are always on the lookout for international talent and it is not unusual for the top teams to be powered entirely by British, Canadian and Australian students recruited especially for their skills on water. Soccer (football) is developing on American shores and good British players are in demand. Cricketers might find themselves out on something of a limb but most standard sports (athletics, tennis, golf, lacrosse) will be represented on campus and they are all crying out for talent.

It may well be that the recruiters will find you first. If you are the World No. 1 in a particular area, or have consistently played for a British junior team, then you should definitely consider viewing your sporting prowess as a potential admissions passport. As all admission forms repeat *ad nauseam*, American colleges are looking for diverse individuals who will allow the school to excel in all fields. Sporting events are huge dates in every school calendar and coaches travel the world to attract the best players.

If you are chasing the ultimate jock dream, you should take note of a few things. Athletes at the top universities are treated royally, but they get away with much less than those in the big public schools. They are expected to maintain high academic levels – and coaches rarely intervene to sort out their schedules. Playing any sport at university level is hard work and juggling this with tough classes can prove difficult. Less rigorous schools place more emphasis on sport, and a star football player is treated as a hero all over campus. But elite colleges have their share of sports groupies as well and both male and female athletes will find that a little bit of lycra or that letterman sweater can get them a long way.

And then there are the financial benefits ...

The US offers great opportunities for talented athletes, and even a cost-free education. The fount of all knowledge is the EAS of the Fulbright Commission – run to them for their literature. What it says in summary is:

Athletic scholarships are awarded for baseball, basketball, crew (rowing), cross-country, fencing, football (American), golf, gymnastics, ice hockey, indoor track, lacrosse, skiing, soccer, softball, swimming and diving, tennis, track and field, volleyball, water polo, women's field hockey and wrestling. Archery, badminton, bowling, equestrian sports and squash have been designated as 'emerging sports' and scholarships in these sports are available to women only in an effort to achieve equality between men's and women's scholarships. Some universities offer martial arts, riflery, rodeo, rugby and sailing, but very few of those will offer these sports on a scholarship basis. Athletic directors and coaches play a central role in award decision-making, so it is important to establish contact with these individuals early in your application process.

Awards vary from a few thousand dollars to nearly $30,000 per academic year. American football, men's and women's basketball, women's tennis, women's gymnastics and women's volleyball awards almost always cover the full cost.

Scholarships are awarded for a year at a time – so going off the rails once you get there is not recommended. To get one you must have recognizable achievements in your sport – check the websites of the universities you are interested in for results of matches or events to see how your ability compares. Different universities set different levels with those in the National Collegiate Athletic Association (NCAA) being the highest. (See *www.ncaa.org* and *www.naia.org*.)

Students with an athletic scholarship must 'meet normal university/college entrance requirements and continue to obtain satisfactory grades in order to receive their scholarships'. These academic requirements are generally nothing to worry about and you often get extra time to complete your degree, but just be aware you can't let the academic ball drop altogether.

To search for scholarships on the internet, go to *http://apps.collegeboard.com/search/advhome.jsp*, click on the icon 'Sports and

Activities', and scroll down to'Sports'. Select the sport you wish to obtain more information about, click on the 'More Detail – Show Sports Level' icon. Tick Division I, etc. and press 'See Results'.

Occasionally coaches visit Europe or see nonUS students at international events. Even if a coach invites you to play for their team, you must still apply to the university through the regular academic application process. Make sure the college will meet your academic as well as your sporting needs. Never go by a verbal agreement on a scholarship, or even by a letter from the coach. Details of the scholarship offer must be written into a contract. A coach can offer an award for one year in the first instance with renewal based on recommendation by the athletics department, which must be approved by the financial aid office. Scholarships are sometimes announced in national and international sporting magazines.

Some students choose to use a placement service instead. Be aware that these services charge a fee, and make sure they have good contacts with US colleges and universities. UK services are listed in the Reference Section at the back of this book.

You can make a direct approach to your sport's coach at individual colleges and universities. You will need to put a sport CV together and the coach may ask for a video demonstrating your abilities. The EAS library can help in this too.

Visas, Immigration and All That Jazz

On the day the acceptance letter drops into your letterbox you might well be deceived into thinking the hard work, struggle and frustration are over. Think again. The toughest application deadline, the most difficult personal essay, the trickiest SAT paper pales into insignificance beside the hardest and most mind-numbingly boring part of admission to the American college experience. The joys of US bureaucracy and the caring immigration system await you. If you are one of those fortunate people blessed with an American parent, passport or green card, stop reading now and count your lucky stars. The rest of you must read on and learn how to deal with the constantly changing visa system, the interminable waits at airports and the work restrictions that will dog your next four years.

International student status

Of course, things are not as bad as they seem. Almost all the big American universities have an International Office set up specifically to help you with these problems. These offices have people on call 24 hours a day and are used to crises of all kinds. When you are accepted to the college, they will send you the paperwork necessary to apply for a visa. This must be obtained from Grosvenor Square –the American Embassy in London. Nowadays there is a compulsory interview for all applicants for student visas. The embassy advises this will take up to four hours, of which approximately three hours and fifty-nine minutes will be spent standing in a queue and sixty seconds spent telling them you are indeed who your passport says you are. Get used to it – this is an experience that will change little over your next four years.

The visa you finally receive will consist of a page in your passport and the accompanying I-20 form. Your name and the most updated version of this form will be registered on all immigration computers. Remember: you must NOT leave your I-20 behind – it is vital for gaining admittance to the country. It is also important you have it authorized at the beginning of your university career by the International Office and then signed each year thereafter.

Things have recently become much more difficult for international students generally – though not so much for UK students – following the tragic attacks of 11 September 2001. Because some of the terrorists involved are believed to have entered the United States on student visas, there has been a clampdown on everyone travelling on one. This has coincided with the arrival of the new SEVIS (Student and Exchange Visitor Information Service) tracking system, which is intended to ensure people enrolled in a university are actually attending that university. It also means the American government has access to personal information about you at all times. While Brits are, for the most part, immune from the hostility of immigration officials, the word among international offices is that these new developments have had a negative impact on the number of international applicants from areas such as the Middle and Far East. It also means fingerprinting and mug shots have become regulation for anyone travelling into the States on a student visa.

What the Americans say ...

Foreign students have always been — and still are — welcome to study in the United States. The tragedy of 9/11 showed the importance of emphasizing national security, but that does not mean we want to discourage legitimate students from coming here to study. We value the diversity and richness they bring to American campuses and society. Although long-standing visa laws and regulations are followed rigorously, and new visa procedures have been introduced since 9/11, the impact on students is always carefully considered.

(Maura Harty, Assistant Secretary of State for Consular Affairs)

Students are subject to the same law as other temporary visitors, and must convince a consular officer that they truly intend to pursue a course of study and will return to their home country when it is over. They must also show they can pay for their education, either from family funds, grants or other sources.

All embassies and consulates worldwide follow a uniform policy about who may be excused from a visa interview. There are few exceptions, and this applies to all non-immigrant visa applicants, not just students. At the direction of Congress, as of October 2005 every visa applicant must offer a biometric identifier that can be encrypted on the visa when issued.

When scheduling visa interviews, all US visa-adjudicating posts now give special consideration to students so they will not miss the opening of the school semester. Many embassies and consulates around the world have opened special windows for students, reducing the wait for interview. Others, where possible, do not require students to have appointments at all.

Some visa applicants, fewer than 2% of the total applying, must wait for Washington to complete an interagency security advisory review, which includes checking all appropriate records. More than 90% of those reviews are completed in less than three weeks.

Students who are studying or working in certain scientific fields may have to wait longer, but security reviews for transfer of technological know-how are not new and were a visa-processing fixture long before 9/11.

Visa policies are designed to maximize security of the United States while encouraging legitimate visitors, including students, to come to this country. The twin goals of secure borders/open door are nowhere more meaningful than in our desire to attract the best students worldwide to the United States. We hope they and their home countries will benefit from the knowledge and outstanding education America's universities can offer the world.

(Maura Harty, Assistant Secretary of State for Consular Affairs)

The facts of the matter ...

Contrary to popular belief, it is no more difficult for UK students to obtain a student visa than in the past. However, the process is more intricate and slightly more expensive. If you are a genuine student and can provide the information requested, you should not experience too much difficulty.

Any student wishing to pursue academic studies in the USA will require a student (F-1) visa. So you can apply, the university which has accepted you will issue a Form I-20 (Certificate of Eligibility for Non-immigrant (F-1) Student Status for Academic and Language Students). You will need to bring this form and the application materials, available from the embassy's website, with you to the interview. Please note: one of the biggest problems, easily avoided, occurs when the name on the form is different from the name in your passport. Make sure that when you begin the application process you use the name that appears in your passport! It is even a good idea to supply a photocopy of your passport with your university application.

In order for the university to have issued you the I-20, the school will have had to enter you in SEVIS so the authorities can monitor you and ensure you are adhering to the conditions of your student visa. Unfortunately, students are charged approximately $100 for this. Some universities have offered to refund this charge to encourage international students, so check and see if your prospective college is one of these.

Once the I-20 is issued and the application completed, you should contact the embassy or consulate and book an interview. All applicants for an F-1 visa must be interviewed. In the course of the interview you will have to submit completed forms and materials, pay the application fee (approximately £60), present your passport with at least one blank page to attach the visa to, provide a passport photo – different size from a UK passport photo – furnish evidence of sufficient funds to cover all expenses including fees while in the US, and provide evidence you will be returning to the UK at the end of your studies.

The evidence needed to demonstrate sufficient funds could include bank statements (yours or your parents), scholarship offers, etc. Please note, it does not necessarily mean you have to have a lump sum sitting in the bank. You simply have to prove, based on account evidence, that you will be able to afford your stay in the US. If your parents are going to assist you, they will have to show statements that demonstrate regular funds will be available.

Perhaps most importantly, you will have to demonstrate you will be returning to the UK. You can do this by demonstrating family links, a home in the UK, and other ties and commitments.

As there are often changes in the procedure, it is best before attending the interview to visit the embassy's website for the most current information, *www.usembassy.org.uk*.

Once the F-1 visa is issued, you may travel to the States, but no earlier than thirty days before your course begins. In the subsequent years of the degree, should you leave the US for a holiday, you will not need to wait until thirty days before the term starts to re-enter. The visa will last for the duration of your studies if there is no deviation. You will be permitted to work on campus or off campus (after completion of your first year of study) under limited circumstances. Generally, during term times, you are allowed to work for twenty hours per week and full time during holidays. (See 'Working On and Off Campus' on page 13.)

Finally, when you have completed your studies, you will be permitted to remain in the US for up to sixty days. However, there is the possibility of extending your stay for up to twelve months following your degree to pursue practical training. For further information regarding working during your degree or training after its completion, please contact your university.

Other Options for Getting to Uni in the USA
Work exchange/internships
A number of programmes between the US and the UK encourage

international understanding through practical work experience (called 'internships' in the US) for up to a maximum of eighteen months. The programmes are known as work exchange programmes, and vary widely in nature, some allowing participants to do any job available, others more restricted to specific fields. Check and see which programme best suits your situation and needs.

Work exchange programmes can only be administered by organizations authorized to issue the US Government form DS 2019. This allows work exchange programme participants to apply for a J-1 Exchange Visitor Visa at a US Embassy, letting them work legally in the US for a certain period.

Plan your participation in a work exchange programme as early as possible. Some programmes require you to obtain an offer of employment in the US before you apply to them. Programmes may have application deadlines or require you to apply a certain number of months before you intend to leave for the US. Check how long the whole process will take. Allow time for the visa application, and if possible do not purchase a flight until you know your application has been successful.

Gap year

For students wanting to take time out before going to university in the UK, it is possible to spend a semester, a year or a summer studying at a US university.

You may find there are more possibilities for gap year study in small, private, liberal arts institutions than in larger state-funded colleges and universities. When you have found universities you are interested in, contact the admissions office for each university, making it clear you will be applying to spend a year in the US before going on to university in the UK. Therefore, you will be applying for 'special' or 'non-degree' student status. It is possible that you will have to fulfil the same requirements as those applying for full degrees.

Studying in the US can be expensive. Tuition ranges between $3,000 and $25,000 for nine months. Cost of living can range between $6,000 and $15,000, depending on the region and your lifestyle. And be warned – there are few scholarships available for short-term study.

The academic year generally begins in late August or early September. If you are only interested in a one semester deal, it is also possible to enrol for the Spring/Winter semester (normally beginning in January).

An alternative is to apply via a placement programme, which may be able to find a place for you and make all the general arrangements. Organizations offering this type of assistance are listed in the Reference Section.

Undergraduate exchange

There are two main ways to study for a short time in the US as part of your UK undergraduate degree: participate in an established study abroad programme through your UK university; or apply directly to the US universities themselves. Generally, programmes run for a summer, semester or entire academic year. It is easier to go with an established exchange programme organized by your UK university than to apply to US universities directly. Exchanges are normally run by the International Office or possibly the American Studies department.

If your UK institution does not have any exchange links with any

US universities, it is possible to contact US universities directly and apply as a non-degree student. This can, however, be complex and time-consuming. You will need to check with your UK institution to see if they will recognize the courses you wish to take at the US institution. If you decide to apply as a non-degree student, then you should read the section above on Gap Year study as many of the criteria there will apply to you in the undergraduate situation.

Funding for international students to pursue one year of undergraduate study in the US is very limited. You may wish to see if a local public library has a copy of the UNESCO guide *Study Abroad* listing sources of funding for US study.

If you find you are not eligible for financial assistance from your UK university or the US university you will be attending, consider approaching multinational companies, local businesses or a Rotary group.

Transferring from part-way through a UK university degree is possible – but talk to the EAS before you do anything else.

A Glossary for the Transatlantic Traveller

'You say tomayyyto and I say tomarrrrto ...'

THE BRITS	THE AMERICANS
Academics	
1st year	Freshman
2nd year	Sophomore
3rd year	Junior
4th year	Senior
Public School	Private School
State School	Public School
Uni	School
Year group	Class (as in 'My class is graduating tomorrow')
Food	
100s and 1000s	Sprinkles
Aubergine	Eggplant
Chips	French Fries
Courgette	Zucchini
Crisps	Chips
Fish Fingers	Fish Sticks
Jam	Jelly
Jelly	Jello
Porridge	Oatmeal
Pudding	Dessert
Tinned	Canned
YOG-hurt	YO-ghurt
Relationships	
Bloke	Guy
Fit	Cute/Hot
Going out	Dating

Mingin'	Gross
Pull	Hook-up
Snog	Kiss

Clothes

Braces	Suspenders(!)
Jumper	Sweater
Trainers	Sneakers
Trousers	Pants
Waistcoat	Vest

In General

'Sorry'	'Excuse Me'
Anti-Clockwise	Counter-Clockwise
Athlete	Jock
Autumn	Fall
Backside/Bum	Fanny/Tushy
Black Tie Dance	Formal
Boot (of car)	Trunk
Brilliant	Awesome
Chemist	Drug Store
Cinema	Movie Theater
Clever	Smart
Condom	Rubber
Fags	Cigarettes (WATCH OUT HERE – 'fag' has only a negative homosexual connotation in the States)
Film	Movie
Flat	Apartment
Football	Soccer
Fringe	Bangs
Full Stop	Period
Gents	Men's Room
Lift	Elevator
Line	Queue
Loo	Restroom/Bathroom
Maths	Math
Mobile	Cell phone

Nappies	Diapers
Nerd	Geek
Pavement	Sidewalk
Petrol	Gas
Post	Mail
Post-code	Zip-code
Pub	Bar
Rubber	Eraser
Rucksack	Backpack
Smart	Well-dressed
Sofa	Couch
Tap	Faucet
Tea Towel	Dish Cloth
Underground/Tube	Subway
Very	Quite (saying that something is 'quite good' or looks 'quite nice' IS a compliment from an American)
Washing Up	Doing the Dishes

And some shops for reference

Abercrombie & Fitch – the epitome of preppy style
Anthropologie – something a little bit funkier
Banana Republic – upmarket GAP but still high-street prices
GAP – as in the UK but MUCH cheaper
J. Crew – a close second in the preppy stakes
Victoria's Secret – some good presents for you and the girlfriend

Some Other Useful Tips

When an American says, 'Hey, what's up?' to you, they do NOT expect a five-minute answer on your cheating boyfriend, overdue paper and aching back. In fact, it is a mere formality – answer with a casual 'Not much'.

American Holidays

President's Day – winter day off school
Spring Break – drunken student debauchery, usually sometime in March
Thanksgiving – late-November turkey celebration

Veteran's Day – Remembrance Day (the only people wearing poppies are Canadians)
Fourth of July – Independence Day

Reference Section

Here are some helpful books and website links to supplement the wisdom we have imparted.

All Aspects of Higher Education in the US

www.educationusa.state.gov
The US Educational Advisory Service
US–UK Fulbright Commission,
Fulbright House, 62 Doughty Street, London WC1N 2JZ
0207 404 6994
www.fulbright.co.uk/eas

They also have offices at Queen's University and the Central Library, Belfast; University of Ulster, Londonderry; University of Edinburgh, University of St Andrews; University of Glasgow; University of Dundee; University of Manchester; University of Wales, Swansea; University of Birmingham; University of Hull; and University of Plymouth.

Travelling in the US

Site to help you plan your trip to the US:

Independent America: *www.independentamerica.com*

Getting a Student Visa
The US Embassy: *www.usembassy.org.uk* and *www.unitedstatesvisas.gov*

Help with the Application Process

The Common Application: *www.commonapp.org*

Education Prep Inc: *www.educationprep.com*
Jon Tabbert Associates: *www.jontabbert.com/jta.htm*

Financial Aid Assistance
General information

www.bunac.org for internships and work exchange

www.collegeboard.com/paying
www.fastweb.com/ib/edupass-21f
www.fdncenter.org
www.globalgrant.com
www.iefc.com

www.iefa.org/public/search.html
www.InternationalStudentLoan.com
www.InternationalScholarship.com
www.scholarships.com
www.scholarshipexperts.com

Foundation Grants to Individuals, 13th edition, The Foundation Center. ISBN 0-1931-9236-5, *www.fdncenter.org.* It is also available as a subscription service. It has a section on International Applications, listing American foundation grants given exclusively to individuals from other than the US.

Peterson's College Money Handbook 2005, 22nd edition, Peterson's, ISBN 0-7689-1503-1, *www.petersons.com.* Everything you need to know: step-by-step explanation of the student financial id process. Complete descriptions of financial aid programmes at more than 1800 colleges and universities. Exclusive chart showing what parents and students actually pay on average at each college.

Scholarship Almanac 2005, 8th edition, Peterson's, ISBN 0-7689-1514-7, *www.petersons.com.* Latest facts and figures on 500 largest scholarships in USA and Canada; ABCs of paying for college; tips on applications procedures; advice on how to estimate college costs.

Athletic scholarships

Consultancy for Overseas Sports Scholarships: *www.firstpointusa.com.* Andrew Kean, Head Sports Consultant, FirstPoint (Europe) Ltd, 200 Bath Street, Glasgow G2 4HG, 0141 572 2005, fax 0141 572 2003, *Andrew@firstpointusa.com*

Educational Advisory Service: *www.fulbright.co.uk/eas/contact/index.html*

Financial Aid for Student Athletes: *www.finaid.org/otheraid/sports.phtml*

Kopia: *www.kopia.org* Kopia LLC, PO Box 30389, Philadelphia, PA19103

National Collegiate Athletic Association: *www.ncaa.org*

National Association of Intercollegiate Athletics: *www.naia.org*

National Junior College Athletic Association: *www.njcaa.org*

NCAA Initial Eligibility Clearinghouse: *www.ncaaclearinghouse.net*

Sports-Ed: *www.sports-ed.com.* Jamie Bennett, 8 Oxford Street, Nottingham NG1 5BH, tel. and fax 0115 941 7715

Sports Scholarships in America placement service: *marva@cpoauk.com*

Sports Scholarships and College Athletic Programmes 2004, 5th edition, Peterson's, ISBN 0-7689-1524-4, *www.petersons.com.* Get advice on winning your share of $500 million in sports scholarships. How to get sports scholarships; details on athletic programmes at more than 1,700 accredited colleges and universities; contact information on coaches and athletic directors; views on what coaches are looking for in college athletes; pros and cons of financing college with an athletic scholarship; current perspectives on college athletics. Colleges are listed alphabetically. The indexes are by sport and also by geography.

Help Choosing a University

The College Board: *www.collegeboard.com/explore/index.html*

Hobson's College View – European Edition: *www.collegeview.com/college/niche/international/europe*

www.lifeintheusa.com Describes just what it says, life in the USA

Peterson's: *www.petersons.com*

Princeton Review: *www.princetonreview.com*

www.universityroadtrips.com Arranges tours for finding a university

www.uscampus.com For every side of living and studying in the USA

Barron's Profiles of American Colleges 2004, 26th edition, Barron's, ISBN 0-7641-75750, *www.barronseduc.com*. In-depth profiles of more than 1,650 schools. Plus Barron's exclusive rating system, a comprehensive index to college majors and a CDRom. It has a section on 'Study in the US' covering areas including admission, finance and application. The College Admissions Selector lists under titles from 'Most Competitive', to 'Non Competitive'. There is an index of college majors linking to a 'Deciding on a Major and Career' section. 'Colleges at a Glance' presents some of the data that initially concerns many students, e.g. environment, size and test scores.

The College Board College Handbook 2005, The College Board, ISBN 0-87447-694-1, *www.collegeboard.com*. Over 3,600 four-year and two-year colleges. 'The only guide to every accredited college in the US'. Indexes colleges by type, special characteristics, e.g. women only, undergraduate enrolment size, admission selectivity, admission/placement policies, college that offer ROTC, NCAA sports.

Colleges are described by state. The section called 'Eight Major Myths' includes 'Liberal arts education = unemployment'.

Colleges for Students with Learning Disabilities or ADD 2003, 7th edition, Peterson's, ISBN 0-7689-1268-7, *www.petersons.com.* Complete profiles of programmes at more than 1,100 colleges in the US and Canada. Programme details on diagnostic testing, orientation and summer programmes, fees and application requirements. Explore unique aids and services. Discover insider advice from the Learning Disability Programme Director.

Four Year Colleges 2005, 35th edition, Peterson's, ISBN 0-7689-1379-9, *www.petersons.com.* Latest information on more than 2,100 four-year colleges and universities in the US and Canada. Plus the inside scoop on private v. public schools, honour calls, ROTC (Reserve Officer Training Corps) programmes and more. It boasts an at-a-glance application checklist to help you get started. Tips on surviving standardized test and searching for scholarships. Newly updates advice for international students. It has an easy to use majors index and entrance difficulty index. Colleges and universities are organized by state.

There are college profiles and then an inside look at nearly 1,000 colleges and universities.

The Princeton Review Complete Book of Colleges 2005, Random House, ISBN 0-375764062, *www.PrincetonReview.com.* Up-to-date information on 1,700 colleges and universities. Uses an icon system to indicate the number of students, cost, environment, intercollegiate athletic division and 'The Best 345 Colleges' – meaning it appears in The Princeton Review book *The Colleges,* where each school has a detailed profile. There is a section to analyse which group of colleges will interest you. It has information on admissions, campus life, financial aid and athletic programmes.

'Rankings' Compilers

www.library.uiuc.edu/edx/rankings.htm University of Illinois, Champaign-Urbana: College of Rankings

www.princetonreview.com/college/research/rankings/rankings.asp
Princeton Review

www.usnews.com/usnews/rankguide/rghome.htm US News and World
Report

General Undergraduate Information About Schools in the US
College search
www.a2zcolleges.com
www.allaboutcollege.com
www.allcampus.com
www.auap.com
www.collegeboard.com
www.collegeconfidential.com
www.collegeispossible.org
www.collegeview.com/college/niche/international/europe
www.collegexpress.com
www.commonapp.org/default.htm
www.co-op.edu
www.educationconnect.com
www.edupass.org
www.globalcomputing.com
www.gocollege.com
www.greekpages.com
www.guideforparents.com
www.iie.org
www.intstudy.com
www.justcolleges.com
www.learn4good.com
www.mapping-your-future.org
www.mycollegeguide.org/index.phtml
www.princetonreview.com
www.sourcebooks.com
www.studyoverseas.com/america/usamain.htm
www.transworldeducation.com
www.univsource.com
www.usjournal.com/en/students/info/fairs.html
www.usnews.com

www.usembassy.org.uk

Sites specifically for community colleges

American Association of Community Colleges: *www.aacc.nche.edu*
National Alliance of Community and Technological Colleges:
admin1.athens.tec.ga.us/nactc.html
US News Online: *www.usnews.com*
US State Colleges, Universities and Community Colleges:
www.50states.com/college

Admission Tests

ACT Board: *www.act.org*
www.fairtest.org For colleges that may exempt from standard tests
SAT Board: *www.collegeboard.com*
TOEFL: *www.toefl.org*

Taking the test

www.ets.org in Princeton and CITO Group SAT Program, PO Box
1109, 6801 BC Arnhem, Netherlands can also arrange registration
www.fulbright.co.uk/eas in London for information on registration,
fees and test centres.

Practising the test

Best College Admission Essays, Petersons. *www.petersons.com*. Fifty sample essays plus tips and advice for writing your own.

The Official SAT Study Guide: For the New SAT 2004, The College
Board, *www.collegeboard.com*. Take eight practice tests and receive
estimated scores. Also read a chapter on the new SAT essay which
includes practice essay questions.
11 Practice Tests for the New SAT and PSAT, The Princeton Review,
ISBN 0-3757-6434-8. *www.PrincetonReview.com*. There is also a series
covering the subject tests.

The Real SAT II: Subject Tests, The College Board. Full-length tests
for every SAT II subject, tips and strategies.
Bonas MacFarlane (Educational Consultants): Charles Bonas, 37
Linden Gardens, London W2 4HQ, 0207 221 8260, *info@bonasmac-*

farlane.co.uk. London consultants with a professional team of advisers and tutors.

Christine, Paul and Associates: 0207 7920243, mobile 07779 354858, *chrispaul@rhone.abel.co.uk.* Private tuition on your own or in pairs on SAT I, SAT II Writing and Math, TOEFL and TOEIC in London with short intensive courses available outside the city. March to December.

Frances King School of English: 5 Grosvenor Gardens, London SW1W OBD, 0207 8706577, fax 0207 3419771, *info@francesking.co.uk.* TOEFL and TOEIC preparation courses. University Placement Service. Accredited by the British Council.

The Hampstead School of English: 553 Finchley Road, London NW2 2BU, 0207 794 3533, fax 0207 431 2987, *jill@hampstead-english.ac.uk.* TOEFL and GMAT courses, one-to-one or classes. Also provides introduction to computer generated testing, library, practice testing and home study assistance.

Kaplan Test Prep: 3-5 Charing Cross Road, London WC2H OHA, 0207 930 3130, fax 0207 930 8009, *London_Center@kaplan.com.* More than 60 years experience and offering a wide range of courses, private tuition and courses, Monday-Sunday. Also www.kaptest.com/uk.

New World Tutoring: Steve Schwartz, 0208 699 3248. GMAT, SAT I and SAT II (writing and math). Private lessons in your home.

The Studyworks: Michele Collias BA(hons) JD (cum laude), 46 Queens Gardens, London W2 3AA, 0207 4029877, fax 0207 2580417. Courses on GMAT-CAT and SAT with review of both the Math and Verbal sections of each exam.

English language tests
www.ielts.org An alternative accepted by many universities
www.toefl.org For TOEFL tests

Applying as a Transfer Student: Credential Evaluators

Educational Credential Evaluators: *www.ece.org*
Educational Evaluators International Inc: *garyee@ix.netcom.com*
Education International Inc: *www.educationinternational.org*
Educational Records Evaluation Service, Inc.: *www.eres.com*
Evaluation Service: *www.eres.com*
Foreign Academic Credentials Service, Inc: *www.facsusa.com*
Foundation for International Services: *www.fis-web.com*
Global Services Associates: *global@iccas.com*
International Consultants of Delaware, Inc: *http://www.icdel.com*
International Education Research Foundation, Inc.:
http://www.ierf.org
Josef Silny and Associates, Inc. International Education
Consultants: *www.jsilny.com*
National Association of Credential Evaluation Services:
www.naces.org
SpanTran Educational Services: *www.spantran-edu.com*
World Education Services, Inc.: *www.wes.org*